THE MEDEAD

Also by Fiona Templeton

Elements of Performance Art (with Anthony Howell)
London
YOU-The City
Delirium of Interpretations
oops the join
Cells of Release
Invisible Dances (with Bock & Vincenzi)
Going (with the Theatre of Mistakes)

THE MEDEAD

AN EPIC OF MEDEA

FIONA TEMPLETON

ROOF BOOKS
NEW YORK

ISBN: 978-1-931824-54-5
Library of Congress Control Number: 2014934112

Cover photo by Paula Court
Author photo by Hugo Glendinning

 This book is made possible, in part, by the New York State Council
on the Arts with the support of Governor Andrew Cuomo and the
New York State Legislature.

Roof Books are distributed by
Small Press Distribution
1341 Seventh Avenue
Berkeley, CA. 94710-1403
Phone orders: 800-869-7553
www.spdbooks.org

Roof Books
are published by
Segue Foundation
300 Bowery
New York, NY 10012
seguefoundation.com

for Mum

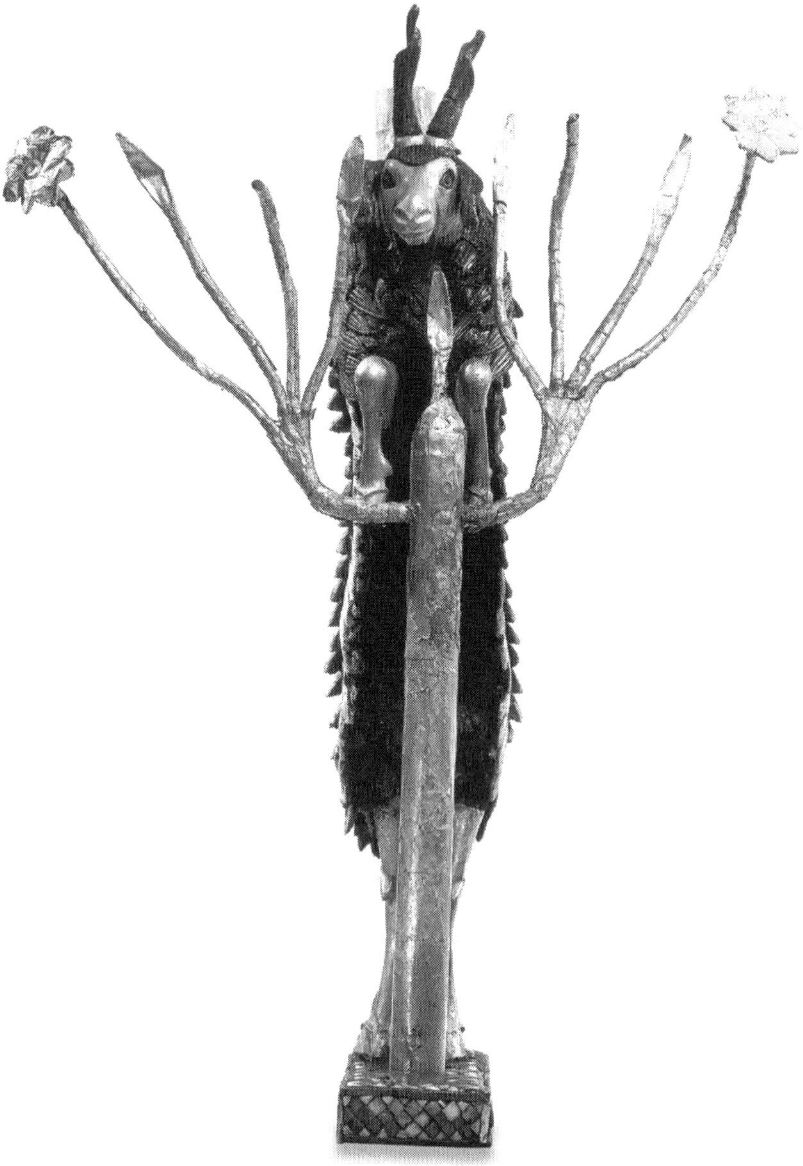

CONTENTS

Valda Setterfield and Nato Murvanidze

MITHER TONGUE

i

Fiona Templeton's current writing practice occupies the edge of the territories, both real and metaphorical, that she has inhabited as a matter of course throughout her long career as a poet and theatre maker. This is writing as uncovering, unearthing, and excavating, picking her way across the foreshore of myth and metaphor for detritus, matching parts of patterns, picking up windblown objects, brushing sand from stones, since it is true that time is material, that the imagination is a place, that maps become garments, that shores become cliffs, that a cut raw edge between two syllables can be repaired with the most everyday, mundane piece of twine, and that conceptual tools can cross that mystical boundary between reality and imaginative construction.

Why cross it at all? Why not live close to the edge but away from it, in the village, not on the cliff that threatens to fall into the sea? Why wander? Why treat language as if it were a midden in which sounds and glyphs and bits of words have rotted together and then split at the seams, forming them into new neighborly communities, non-linear, centred in female experience? Many women writers have occupied these dangerous spaces over the years. Some have cast themselves as archaeologists of long-buried folklore, turning over the soil of story, spinning new meanings from old straw. Ursula Le Guin, Mary Daly, Marina Warner, Adrienne Rich, Kathy Acker, Anna Kavan, Angela Carter, Christa Wolff are among the many fabulists, philosophers and poets who have set up camp on the edge of myth and language, and who have reported from this frontline. Who knew that Templeton would set her own camp of witness here, in the middle of such well worn ground, thick with the old bedding of others? Who knew that this poet would choose to re-hear the signals, re-make the old women-and-language terms? Who knew she would take on Medea?

ii

The Medead is concerned with the mythic roots of language, and the associations of women's speech.

Language, like light, makes the invisible become visible,
covers its invisible contours, gives it form, its own form.

The journey of origin that the writing itself undertook began in Templeton's own journey to the Black Sea coast, where Medea herself emerged from language and became figured. As she writes in her afterword to this book, Medea begins in Hyperborea, or, before the dawn, a word embodying the ancient Greek idea of far north. *Medead* is a name collapsed and extended in one. It is also 'me dead,' a figure engaged on an epic journey, a 'night sea crossing' as Templeton outs it, a descent of the soul, a going down, a ferrying.

Templeton takes the most basic and ubiquitous of forms, the journey story, and extracts its governing drives. Like a previous generation of radical feminist spinners of word-forms Templeton takes a stand for the primacy of language in shaping the world of experience and in constructing female subjectivity—over a lifetime. The subject of women's language and women's rage has picked up some cultural dirt on its long journey to this particular surface. It has the patina of the collective, of the hands that have passed it through. In Templeton's hands it achieves that most unlikely of qualities, delicacy and even humor. How can it be that this windblown sheaf of subjects, the ageing female body, the death of children, mourning, utter loss, should be so imbued? Yet it is. It has to be.

iii

Of course there is a background, a logic, a tradition behind this ambulatory practice of hers. She walks over crushed shells. Experimental performance has long been a nourishing host for women artists and writers and poetic makers of all sorts, and it has been strewing its remains and its riches around for anyone who comes after to use. Yet it is still unsettling territory, hard to make one's way over, necessarily beyond the pale. Templeton moves carefully, upturning sediment. Her movement is, of course, rooted in her autotopography: the story of, the place of, her history as a writer across worlds.

iv

Templeton's work moves through multiple languages and dialects, creating her own canon of association. A Scot travelling in English, she is open to the movement of terms between close linguistic neighbors—after all, Scotland itself houses two historic national cultures, Braid Scots and Gaelic, each jostling for space against the imposition of a southern dialect of English, the dominant institutional language of Scotland from the seventeenth century. To be a writer born into Scots is to juggle spoken and literary forms. How to speak is a question that has absorbed and challenged Scots poets and writers from Robert Burns to Hugh MacDiarmid to the present Scots Makar (poet laureate) Liz Lochead. The women have answered it in various ways. 'Gin I'm a livan tongue, loe me,' wrote Edith Anne Robertson in 1955.

Aware of her distance from the centre, Templeton left for New York in 1979, and has lived in two continents ever since. She is not part of the new canon of Scots writers; not part of the careful, observant lyric enquiry of Kathleen Jamie, or the bravura, bloody minded grit of Liz Lochead. She shares more with Scotland's greatest twentieth century poet, Edwin Morgan, who also wrote across languages, translating *Beowulf* and *Macbeth* into Scots (as well as Racine, Montale, Mayakovsky and many others), curating visual poetry, always, always crossing lines.

Templeton took that most traditional of Scots decisions, migration westwards. If there was ever anywhere to go, historically, it was to that far, far bigger island out across the Atlantic, past the outlying isles, past Iona and Mull, past Uist, Harris and Lewis and St. Kilda, with their Norse remains, their Norse names, their trails of light settling, housing the offerings of those ancient travelers wending their way up the coast of Scotland. In America the language is different, the potential is different, it is an *other* English. Templeton came to America as a performance maker rooted in avant-garde practice, decidedly non-mainstream, committed to alternate ways of putting together visual and linguistic meaning. In America she began her life as a writer, making landfall amongst a constellation of women language poets each writing from consciously unsettled, untethered places. In America, poetic second language plays, mixing it up, worrying the terms on which poetry is made, rubbed up against ideas about what it means, and has meant, to be a woman poet, interested not in lyric but in language's forms — America gave Templeton room to breathe.

She is, therefore, part of a transatlantic conversation, a maker whose de-centredness allows me to see her as kin to other world writers in inflected English, such as Nicole Brossard in Canada, or Debbie Tucker Green and Caroline Bergvall in the UK — and, thinking back, to Gertrude Stein herself — each of whom writes across the historical timespan of English as it moves across continents, dragging its prehistories, and its colonial peregrinations, with it. Alongside her, connected by traversing paths, run the traces of other footprints: writers Monique Wittig and Nathalie Sarraute; artists such as Louise Bourgeois, Eva Hesse, Susan Hiller, Carolee Schneemann; film-makers Chantal Ackerman, and Maya Deren, poets Rae Armantrout, Carla Harryman, Susan Howe, Hannah Weiner. Each of these is a woman artist concerned with animate form. But while Templeton has many elective affinities with poets whose work operates across boundaries of language, or that use language's sonic, visual and performative properties, she is, perhaps unusually, also a performance writer in an *oracular* tradition, almost a bardic tradition that she has adapted to her use. The spoken, oracular, declamatory form that she uses in *The Medead* is also a prophetic voice of warning, a cry from the body, through the figure of a woman demented by oppression.

> o face
> too hot
> two handle
> too cool

> to king
> with a blow
> and more unarming a head in rescue
> facing
> drown deaf, grown, death, affront confront me

v

I think of her on this day, today, when she is on one side of the Atlantic, and I on another. I see a line that helps me to connect the pieced fragments, the transforming elements, of her practice, and it is a line of biography. It isn't necessarily *her* biography; it is more a skein of threads, a skein of moving paths as the work follows the movement of terms, languages and etymologies, which in turn become figures as they move. The writer moves along the border between practices, picks up what is strewn there, that cannot be found anywhere else, and works it in. This is the root of *The Medead*. It moves off from here.

> mother: yes, well, what Medea really means; med- as also in medusa means guardian, ruler, caretaker; from Sanskrit MA meaning measure, thus our mathematics, measure as from a center rather than linear, thus also metra (womb) as well as metre; Medea probably also contains dea, goddess; also the actress playing Ideia becomes the oldest Medea; v also southern U.S. term for mother M'dea, for mother-dear; I also wonder about the etymology of the "me"- part In Georgian mother is "dada" ! and grandmother didideda, "my mother" = mideda. Medea's mother 's name "Ideia" (see "skin" above) is both appearance as beauty, shape, visibility as seen, and a first coming.
> (directing notes for *The Medead*)

There she goes, digging up those long ago migrated, buried and hidden meanings, not *like* mineral seams but *actually* mineral seams brought into the light: amalgam, conglomerate, fossil thick, possible, ancient. Nothing stays her still. Her mither tongue is as fluid and changing as the foreshore, but *still* it is her tongue. Still there is the mither. Still the tongue is rooted in the throat. Still there is the body of the mother at the root of all language learning.

vi

Down to the ground; down to the ground. The idea that writing itself might be a country to which an artist travels, and which she might occupy, is a continuing trope. It crosses genres, it comforts, it enables and it provides a kind of hope.

12

Glancing at the map of Templeton's work, as if seen from above, I pick out the major sites of her public performance works as three constellations, speckled around with smaller sites. Running from and around them are the traces of deeper, older lines of language and meaning: whirled, vernacular, clear. These three sites constitute the territory of her practice since 1979: *You -The City, Cells of Release, The Medead,* Each is in conversation with the others. Produced over a period of thirty years, it is not so much that the earlier work leads onward to the next instance, more that the works occupy a commons to which the writer is able to bring equivalent tools, and to re-use approaches, the better to enlarge and articulate her vision.

In her earlier large-scale works, *You—The City* and *Cells of Release*, the sites of city and cell were each explored in public, witnessed, performances. The presence of the writer/maker enabled a conversation with participants, and in the case of *Cells of Release*, with inhabitants both past and present. In *The Medead* the trope has been reversed. There is no specific site; instead the work is grounded in the mythic body of the mother. From here, it moves back into theatre space. *The Medead* is the re-collection of a journey that becomes a web of meaning that becomes a figure that becomes that has always been, mother, tongue, speech, manifestation. Its process of making can be seen as the embodiment of multiple journeys. As performance, Templeton imagines the work moving through a theatre space, around the viewers. It reminds us of the body's part in the dynamic process of engaging with art.

vii

The tools Templeton uses in her journey are older now, they are tempered with use. This work returns to some of the earliest signals of human culture, as if they are now faint radio pulses from far in the universe. It reminds us of the dust from which we are made: shards of meaningful sound. In taking us on a journey to the root of the tongue, it suggests a length of temporal attention that goes beyond us. This is life-work, late life-work. This is how you save your life; narrate your times; through operating at the forming edge of where you are, and reporting what you are finding. No need to tell your own tale, just call out what's there. Of course death is present, of course. The record starts here, in the mither tongue.

This much I know: she keeps her ear to the ground. She listens, she speaks, she writes, and I respond.

Claire MacDonald
September 2013

On reading the play:

The columns are simultaneous across the double page spread, as in the staves of music but vertically. So the spoken Text (2nd column to the right) reads straight from the top of that column to the bottom and continues on the next page. Chorus and text interrupt each other if the text visually interrupts on the page.

The left column (Directions) refers to what is actually happening on stage. This can be different to what any narration by the chorus (far right column) would imply. Though they many have things in common, the second is not merely a theatrical representation of the first nor the first an explanation of the second. The two columns tell different interpretations. Sometimes these two columns may be contradictory, the audience not hearing the same as they are seeing. There are also some bird instructions in bold in the Birds columns.

The Chorus is always spoken by more than one person, except where marked. In general, it should be clear that Chorus and Birds are not characters as such, though occasionally the Chorus are a group such as neighbors, sailors etc as in the text. The Chorus narrates or drives the action, and is spoken according to the same timing rules as the Text (see below). The Birds, however, comment on the action, in parallel with the Text and Chorus.

In the Chorus column, some lines are in bold – these are spoken as scene titles. Orpheus says all of them once he has become a character (even after he is dead); before that they are shared across the performers. The exception is Part 4, Medea in Corinth, in which Medea says all of her own titles. There are also a couple of exceptions when Orpheus is mentioned in the title.

Timing

On the page, the flow of the stanzas in the text does not necessarily break for a new speaker, and sometimes breaks within one speaker. These are rhythmic markers, and the text should be spoken accordingly.

Line breaks are also rhythmic markers, and should not be over-elided to "naturalize" the speech. A double line break is a longer pause.

Birds – 3 colums

1. The first Bird column has the birds most backgrounded or most continuous. As they fade into the background they are in lighter text.

2. The second Bird column shows birdsong phrases. These may be (randomly?) *repeated*. They should be quieter than the main speeches unless specified. For repeated phrases: for example, if a bird line is written "pick it up pick it up", then the *double* repeat of "pick it up" is the phrase to be repeated, with a breath or longer break between each *double* repeat. If only "pick it up" were written, the breath or break would come between each single occurrence

3. The third Bird column shows lines that should come in are at *specific points*; these may be more prominent.

All birds may also pick up on phrases or fragments spoken by the characters, and repeat them *in the same cadence*. They occur differently in each scene (see directions for the scene).

Characters

in Aia: **Medea, Aeetes**, her father, king of Colchis; **Ideia**, her mother. Non-speaking,
  may be played by chorus: **Apsyrtus**, her brother; **Chalkiope**, her sister
Argonauts: **Jason**, a clever young Greek hero; **Orpheus**, a poet and mystic;
other men on the voyage: **Medea**, the nurse(s) of Dionysos, **Makris**; other women;
Libya, the place (a woman) in Iolcos: **Medea, Jason**, now older; **Aeson**, Jason's
father; **Pelias**, usurper of Jason's father's throne; **Alcestis**, Pelias' daughter;
  Admetus, her husband, for whose death she substitutes her own
in Corinth: only **Medea** but she also satirises **Glauke**, Jason's new wife-to-be
in Athens: **Medea, Aegeus**, king of Athens; **Theseus**, his son
returning to the east: one live **Medea**, one on film; plus all at a certain point
in heaven: **Medea, Achilles**, the Greek old-style physical hero
Chorus, Birds throughout

Roles

Characters not involved in the main action of a scene remain onstage as chorus or birds. The characters are distributed as follows:

girl: Medea in Aia, Alcestis,
young woman: Medea on Argo
youngish woman: Medea in Iolcos
woman: Medea in Corinth
mature woman: Medea in Athens, Libya
older woman: Ideia, Medea
  returns the east, and in heaven,
  Makris the nurse of Dionysos

man: Jason, Achilles
youngish man: Admetus, Theseus

mature man: Orpheus

older man: The four fathers:
Aeetes, Aeson, Pelias, Aegeus

LIST OF SCENES

Prologue: Medea in the garden
- Child Medea faces night to guard the door of sunrise

ACT I Part 1—Medea in Aia
- Medea sings a skin of language over the invisible
- her father the eagle, son of the sun
- Medea waits to be a woman
- strangers in the house
- Orpheus offers the trousseau of knives in exchange for Medea's weapons
- the story she didn't know she knew
- the feast
- how the nightingale, orphaned of her tongue by her sister's husband, wrote in scarlet thread, and how the women served him his son
- Medea looks at Jason
- Jason looks at Medea
- Aeetes sets the conditions for the fleece
- Medea's sleepless night of choosing
- Medea digs up the herb of invincibility on the night hill for Jason
- Aeetes leads Jason to the bullring of task
- Medea lulls the fleeceguarding dragon for Jason
- plunder to the sea
- Medea watches her coast recede, her father fly after
- the sea surrounds and disperses, like the limbs of her brother Apsyrtus pursuing

Part 2—Medea on the Argo
- the Black Sea
- the ship sails up the river into the land of wolves
- ice in the blood
- Medea's lullaby beyond the dawn
- Medea wants a child in winter
- the ship emerges into the Mediterranean
- Medea wants a child in spring
- Orpheus tries to drown out the sirens
- Medea rejuvenates the nurses of Dionysos on the island of the sickle
- let none put asunder
- Medea wants a child in summer
- a storm blows the Argo into the Libyan desert

Part 3—Medea in Iolcos
- the arrival of the fleece in the land where the sun dies

- how Jason had come down Mount Pelion after learning he was not the child of the manhorse
- Medea in Jason's father's house
- Orpheus splits
- Medea rejuvenates Jason's father
- Jason and Medea through the door
- Alcentis, later rejected from hell in disgust by Persephone for thinking her life not worth her husband's, tries to rejuvenate her father Pelias
- the tyrant Pelias will not be rejuvenated
- Pelias' family have denied Medea a home, Jason a house

ACT II Part 4—Medea in Corinth
- Medea's bed
- Medea bred
- Medea's head
- Medea's red
- Medea said
- Me dead
- Medea sheds
- Medea's stead

Part 5—Medea in Athens
- Aegeus offers asylum in return for rejuvenation
- Theseus shows up
- Theseus will found the first democracy on the corpse of the body politic
- 3 motives for Aegeus' rejuvenation
- Aegeus recognizes his own hilt as Theseus draws his sword to carve
- Medea takes the heat
- How Ariadne swung above the bull-dance, how Theseus took her cord to get out of a tight maze, how he abandoned her on an island, and how he forgot not to kill his father

Part 6—Medea returns to the east
- The spiral turns the other way
- Medea in Africa
- Medea in Troy
- The catalogue of cloths
- Medea in Persia
- Medea in Colchis
- Medea in Aia   (& FILM: Wandering the map of tears)

Epilogue: Medea in heaven
- the marriage of tears

Stephanie Silver

THE MEDEAD

PROLOGUE

The staging of the Prologue and Act I, Part 1 takes place with audience and performers sharing the flat performance area.

The play begins when the audience enter the performance space preferably from at least two different entrances. No instructions are given as to where they place themselves and the lighting is very low so that the boundaries of the space on all sides are dark.

The performers (entire cast) are placed around the space in such a way that when audience hear them make the sounds (breathing, birds) they are discouraged from finding a specific edge to settle at.

The few lines of the Prologue may be played by an additional very young performer.

Sounds begin in dark, just breathing at first as in sleep, for some time, then a bird or two.

A dim light follows the youngest Medea as she enters like a sleepwalker. She crosses the space more than once, groping, moving behind groups, etc., again to destabilize their understanding of a division of performance area and audience area.

	(Breathing:)		
Gradually we see,	haaaaaaaaaaaaa		
light brightening all	hhhhhhhhhhhhh		
the way up to a flash	aaaaaaaaaaaaaa		
then slowly back	hhhhhhhhhhhhh		
down. This diastole	aaaaaaaaaaaaaa		
and systole of light	hhhhhhhhhhhhh		
happens a few times,	aaaaaaaaaaaaa		
like speeded up	hhhhhhhhhhhhh	who who who	
cycles of day and	aaaaaaaaaaaaa	who who	
night, slowing at	hhhhhhhhhhhhh	sweet?	
almost dark again.	aaaaaaaaaaaaaa	who who who	
It will eventually	hhhhhhhhhhhhh	who who	
lighten again in the	aaaaaaaaaaaaaa	sweet?	
course of the scene,	hhhhhhhhhhhhh		
as of a night. The	aaaaaaaaaaaaaaa	it's you it's you	
breathing goes on	hhhhhhhhhhhhh	it's you	
longer than	aaaaaaaaaaaaaa	it's you it's you	
represented here,	hhhhhhhhhhhhh	it's you	
while the audience	aaaaaaaaaaaaaa		
comes in.	hhhhhhhhhhhhh		
	aaaaaaaaaaaaaa		see
	hhhhhhhhhhhhh		see
	aaaaaaaaaaaaa		
	hhhhhhhhhhhh		
	aaaaaaaaaaaaa		
	hhhhhhhhhhhhh		
	aaaaaaaaaaaaaa		
	hhhhhhhhhhhhh		
	aaaaaaaaaaaaaa		
	hhhhhhhhhhhhh		
	aaaaaaaaaaaaaa		
	hhhhhhhhhhhhh		
	aaaaaaaaaaaaaa		
	hhhhhhhhhhhhh		
	aaaaaaaaaaaaaa		
	hhhhhhhhhhhhh		

Chorus,
a word each: **Child Medea faces night to guard the
                   door of sunrise**

Medea (child):   the moon rounds
                   to meet herself
                   banding
                   the night together

                   .

                   licked bud of her
                   night-blood blue
                   touchable
                   in my doorway

                   .

                   let the dark
                   star awhile

                   ~~

aaaaaaaaaaaaaa
hhhhhhhhhhhhh
aaaaaaaaaaaaaa
hhhhhhhhhhhhh
aaaaaaaaaaaaaa
hhhhhhhhhhhhh
aaaaaaaaaaaaaa
hhhhhhhhhhhhh
aaaaaaaaaaaaaa
hhhhhhhhhhhhh
aaaaaaaaaaaaaa
hhhhhhhhhhhhh
haaaaaaaaaaaaa
hhhhhhhhhhhhh
aaaaaaaaaaaaaa
hhhhhhhhhhhhh
aaaaaaaaaaaaaa
hhhhhhhhhhhhh
aaaaaaaaaaaaaa
hhhhhhhhhhhh
aaaaaaaaaaaaaa
hhhhhhhhhhhhh
aaaaaaaaaaaaaa

swhet sweet sweat
'swet s'wet
swets wets
whets

hhhhhhhhhhhhh
aaaaaaaaaaaaaa
hhhhhhhhhhhhh
aaaaaaaaaaaaaa
hhhhhhhhhhhh
aaaaaaaaaaaaaa
hhhhhhhhhhhhh
aaaaaaaaaaaaaa
hhhhhhhhhhhhh
aaaaaaaaaaaaaa
hhhhhhhhhhhhh
aaaaaaaaaaaaaa
hhhhhhhhhhhhh
aaaaaaaaaaaaaa
hhhhhhhhhhhh
aaaaaaaaaaaaaa
hhhhhhhhhhhhh

she listens — (placed left margin)

SPEAKERS	TEXT	CHORUS

Chorus:
a word each:

**Medea sings a skin of language over
the invisible**

Medea:

it's my song
see where it charts now
the walling time
of my body's letting
into touch
out of cool relations
soon too soon
day will lean on me
I've seen its sheath
I made it
hot-drop forged
and seamless
my lips
fib not
my tongue
is whet
with

answer
from the place

.

tintinnabulus
fabulous infinite
billy bell boo-late
bulb of us
playmate
stalked in woods
jeering years
mind out of watch
of nightingales blowing
restored to pieces
hung in trees
a scape
from land
and cage

.

out here

DIRECTIONS	BIRDS
	aaaaaaaaaaaaaaa
	hhhhhhhhhhhhh
	aaaaaaaaaaaaaaa
	hhhhhhhhhhhhh
	aaaaaaaaaaaaaaa
	hhhhhhhhhhhhhhh
	aaaaaaaaaaaaaaa
	hhhhhhhhhhhhhhh
	aaaaaaaaaaaaaaa
	hhhhhhhhhhhhhhh
	haaaaaaaaaaaaaa
	hhhhhhhhhhhhhhh
	aaaaaaaaaaaaaaa
As she reaches the	hhhhhhhhhhhhhhh
last image, the light	aaaaaaaaaaaaaaa
opens out very slowly,	hhhhhhhhhhhhhhh
then with a flash,	aaaaaaaaaaaaaaaa
dawnlike, behind.	hhhhhhhhhhhhhhh
	haaaaaaaaaaaaaaa

Her father appears.
(image of man-eagle
from Assyria). Bird-
sounds flurry up   (this very morning
from his line, all at   this very duty)
once different song.   (why should you
Chorus is louder.   why should you)
                   (it's so easy to tear)

She starts to fall

Falls

Dawn chorus   (look at you look
             at you)
             (on your feet)
             (pick it up pick it up)
             (toy toy)

change is a pied puffball
pattering
underfoot
the more's the crime
age

well I'll deal daedal de
singing over

it's a winding tongue
a pansyment
a staunch and shuttle
between two poles
we're covering ground here
a slow flap of wound
till plying back
my song draws tight
with night again

See gold night wood's coat ignite.

Aeetes: See the cold gold ram in the tree.

Chorus: birds birds the word birds flies around

M (child):   My wake
Aeetes: Wake up,
M (child):   is done.
Aeetes: it's dawn.

~~

Valda Setterfield and Robert Kya Hill

THE MEDEAD—ACT I
PART 1—MEDEA IN COLCHIS

This part continues the use of space as in the Prologue, i.e.
performers moving among and moving the audience, but lights,
text, birds, and performer movements are used to continually
change the configuration of the audience in the space: e.g.
leaving a small or large performance area; later a division into
Argonauts and Aians; members of the feast; and, in general,
a sense of participating in the events of the narrative and/or
the event of the performance.

Title a word each:

                         (sounds in the

light remains up

                            cadence of

                            the voices,

                            sparsely)

(the chorus reference
is to A, then M)

                    ssssssssssssssssss   b-b-b
                      ssssssssssssssss   b-b-b
                      ssssssssssssssss
                      ssssssssssssssss   *ks,ks*
                      ssssssssssssssss
                      ssssssssssssssss
                      ssssssssssssssss
                      ssssss

Chorus: Medea's father the eagle, son of the sun

Medea: do you know what this is it's shedding its bark
                 like a child
                 I've seen it dissolve in the green woods

Aeetes: no skill
Chorus: tearing apart
Aeetes: confusion
Chorus: waving
Aeetes: no delf decked animal
                 like us
Chorus: he's coughing too much
Aeetes: take this aside away from Port Authority

Chorus: but she did not
Medea: what's on it building up to it by ladder
                 and all too focused on this springing from

Chorus: and in his house
                                              biding
                                           bidding
                                      symptoms
                                      xcese, cease
                                        sheep, ram
                                           armour
                                  perverse peace
Medea: father tease
Chorus: an eagle goes out of the basket
                             flies away over the snails
Aeetes: just intuitive me
                 like she was wax melt away
                 and gently kindly
                 and boldly where it's polished
                 struck away
Chorus: so leans into his neighbour's tomb

"what" and "who"
in this scene are
crows, louder, said
once only

take like rat that   what?

beaked picked
pested   what?

they meet in
the sky   what?

times terrible   what?

brilliant brilliant
brilliant

ah!

what?

SPEAKERS	TEXT	CHORUS
Aeetes:	tiger have pity	
1 Chorus:		what did you say?

Aeetes:

decide
whose is
nice neat
heap o bodies junk
eyelash wound
seize day heart
arm time

scatter homages
dotage
insor
alti
nice
nece
outside me
zone concocted

I know nesce
enough
but wars enough
is clean enough for you
clear is not the day

old man
I'm mapping mine in time
look
in place

Aeetes: we seize flight
oh wings body

Medea: I'm seized hold
a lion oh ah

Aeetes: I'm lift
your feather else

slaying rotor
wings

who?

your soaring
engineer

dark

locked. up. out of
the air

She is turning   sh-sh

sh-sh
dye
blue dye

nothing you knew

Medea:	goodness me, we're so, spinning	
Aeetes:	spines	
Chorus:		cuts familiarities
Aeetes:	did I have I asked you?	
Medea:	I'm seizing too soon	
Aeetes:	angle body to the dregs	
Medea:	fright dazzles away	
Aeetes:	stop crying	
Medea:	who is?	

Aeetes:	we are	

Medea:	you're dried	

Aeetes:	just as hard to be with me as any	
Chorus:		created fingers feathers away
Medea:	that stair wasn't there before the bale has civilized	
Aeetes:	I'm dark	

Chorus:		it's the awful difference seen at the same time

~~

Chorus:	**Medea waits to be a woman**

Medea:	shed shed to be able to say it too young to dye to illaborate blue sky

all Ms just this line:	swathes is us emption painless whose ordinary lives into lead leaning save us

in the forest
muster

here she is
crowds here
she is into here
she is

J unseen by M says   and do we? we're   and do we? we're
bird line stronger   wary   wary
with others

Orpheus appears
unseen by M,
listening   sp-sp

hocu.   pocu

each call other's   in the woods
name   silence stirred

Birds re O   reared its head

fruit heard flower
seen songs

and she what she
what she what
she what she
Orpheus whispers: what she would
birds whispering: and she what   do we? do we?
she what she
would

homes truth
ruth
marrangement
too light to cry

settlement like a seizure
all fall down

locked off
what not done
forked tongs
what late
o, breath, writing
warp speaking
whose saving
incountenance
trying against hocu-pocu
effortless manchomale

Jason
then
Orpheus: **Orpheus, Jason**

Medea: he runs his hand along the bars
and the fence turns into music
I made both of them
the fence and the music

my hand opens
the sun is a rose
soaking the sky
this is the door of my morning

~~

Orpheus: **strangers in the house**

Medea: whispoicitry
a coward
go, go in any room

we do   we do

O&J as if the birds,
but visibly:

sure sure sure
    sure sure sure
    sure sure sure

all: Oh!   Oh!   oh!

song song song
    sing sing

st
st

st   st

what do you imagine
it's the harm off
it's me little beasts
I'm valentine I'm sitting there

the hell-gold reparator
and teasing light
Orpheus: with a voice like a knife
Jason: the jewel in the words
O&J: I'll take it

Medea: not quite all is tame
not quite backwards
and up
as squarely in the face as a flower
looking down
tendrils growing
pistils stamen
a heavenly same heart
no blame
incitement
a parent copy
and calylaughing

Jason &Medea: a fissure

Orpheus: I don't ask her
Jason: will you walk into my trouss   oh
O/M/Ch: oh
Medea: it's a gale
it's a veil of catalogues
a catalogue of knives
staring me in the face

I see   I want   I return
age not far enough
but make its request
lastly   little things
don't be ingenuous
leaves are striking and stead

~~

Orpheus and Jason approach.

birds whisper:

just stand there in
the thicket

you *would*
you would

see it see it

Orpheus: **Orpheus offers the trousseau of knives in exchange for Medea's weapons**

Medea: here let me have it
I can't see it for the trees
Orpheus: dear child
let me inch a breadth of it
let me see it in hell
Medea: take it away
knives are dark
song is old
song is new
that's the description
where I'm tied
like a blade
eat it

this one's firstfeather
ought to be new
more's said
not unlikely yellowfeather
tricking blade
into his moustrous
ear

Medea: I'm afraid I can't follow you
sir size
re J: but there's a reather else
a new opeyes
to J: and come to the gate
the sweet lilacs
hang
a nest gapes
put your hand in
Jason: no I'm such a blade believer
it's a lap
I know what size
I'm share
and seed century

Orpheus: now I'll tell this one

ocu
phew

this title whispered:

*Note: the "story" is
an optional scene; to
omit, drop this title
and skip from after
"glean, curl" to "in
these draperies"*

*M seems to take
something from O,
& addresses her
hand as a mirror:*

using the hand/

whose?
you are

it's looking backwards
and you can carry it
sure-footed across

this one's used in hunting
ook
phew what a fortune

cuthanded
cutheadedlooped through
carving
across
heroes froth

Medea: I'm unpredicted
I'm attracted to the world
I'm a volute
I'll use voice

~~

F Chorus: **the story she didn't know she knew**

Orpheus: it's a late blade
it's pored with light
only the tail protrudes
it's infret
and gorgeon longing
Medea: in whose body was it workplace

Jason: crystal photograph
headshed shining

gorgeous disguise
upending our ownlessness
arms in hand
zero me in fill

*M to her
left hand:*   terrafamilias
orgeous
whose hiding?

41

mirror as a puppet

the turning her head
from side to side
increases in
exaggeration
through the scene.

me you
me us

b-b-b-b-b-b-b-b-
b-b-b

h-h-h-h-h-h-h-
h-h-h-h-h-

h   h-

h-h-h-h
h-h-h-h

ie J says 1st word, M
2nd, then same O&M

stars, starl
rl, rl

ti
dr
yl
sy
rs

M is now playing
between her two
hands like two
characters.

we are

Jason's actions
mirror those of her
hands ie as if he is
one of them in
relation to her.

mether

SPEAKERS	TEXT	CHORUS
Medea:	you are	
M to left:	I'm memusing met us me you bend words bind words	
Medea: *M to left:*	beehives himself if it didn't ear right the first time havoc head bea med in mother	
Medea: *Orpheus:*	I'm head heap hearing and she's	
Jason: *J then M:* *O then M*	million stars, starl glean, curl	
M to left:	alti tress andr-eams pyl-on rosy-aceous tersmile long aldread	
Medea:	stop crying	
M to left:	who is?	
M to right: *Medea:*	we are who are you?	
M to left:	I'm not obviously your father or your brother or your lover or your sister or your mother or your rose that's a circle I'm mether	

starrer

st

st

hhhhhhhhhhhh
  hhhhhhhhhhhh   h
  hhhhhhhhhhhh
  hhhhhhhhhhhh
  hhhhhhhhhhhh
  hhhhhhhhhhhh
  hhhhhhhhhhhh
  hhhhhhhhhhhh
  hhhhhhh

ie man is

**M stands with hands
facing each other.**

SPEAKERS	TEXT	CHORUS

SPEAKERS   TEXT   CHORUS

O & Chorus:
                                                   starrer
                                                   readful
                                                  fingerlips

M to left: strange you find me
tricky

stranger turning
from me
I'm more here than you

M to right: your rearing fair gaze sizes me up

you're what sees
my side

M to left: I'm not your breather
I'm your discovered
hold me size
reather before it's too late
it's too late
I'm wreathing ersize

Orpheus: windswiped eyes
cutting in
like an intelligence

Chorus: the woman looks back at the
                                       man overcome by looking

M to right: o face
too hot
two handle
too cool
to king
with a blow
and more
umarming a head

M to left: drown deaf, grown, death, affront
confront me.

Medea: earth breath
askance jewel

45

claps

mesh

other

whether

ither, whother,
neather

st
sheathings

st

you do

you're me

don't we

M turns the way she   hold that hollow
faced in the   light
prologue, then at J   hope so let it slip

SPEAKERS	TEXT	CHORUS

         the boygirl
         slipping
         on the tongue
         from one breathkin

Chorus/O:
                                a radical edge
                        shocked into being
        cradled at the intersection

Medea: I'm meas
         uring

M to left: other

M to right: whether

Medea: I'm daughter
         I'm held away

M to self: where's my
         duncecap
         in my
         headache

Chorus/O:
        brain bruit unmistakable
              bright shethings
                    by her
                      left
                strokehand

M to left: cares?

M > right: you do

M to left: you're me

M >right: don't we?

M to left: look the other way

Chorus: so that hell can see

Orpheus: in these draperies
         unfold my suggestion
         a small blue bird

running away:

it grows dark

with yellow tear-arrows
its head moving quicker
than a cry
let it fly
away again

Medea: it's my song

they spied on us
that's all I can say

~~

firelit

**Medea has run to her
mother, Ideia**

**There are almost no
birds in these interior
scenes (until M's
sleepless night), so
all speak chorus)**

not spoken:

THE MEDEAD—ACT I

PART 1 B

Orpheus: **the feast**

Ideia: let's give them a taste of our
mediland
inside out

Chorus: hesitating in the threshold from the kitchen
cloth in hand
succeed like fire
ram fix

Ideia: charm harm away

Chorus: cream deputy

Ideia: what to give
to forget
that you don't know

Chorus: sports-cake

Ideia: in the bursting earth

Chorus: a tablecloth is covered with animals
not drawn or embroidered but real
dyed with prescription
poured off

Ideia: he could lay his
adamhand to it

Chorus: she spends
it on to the plate with two spoons

Ideia: into a curve of balance and mellodon
fleece lambswool open plan

Chorus: armfuls
thighs of egg-plants
their tiny minds out of
walnuts
fingers in pistils
fingers in marigold

Medea: like hear music from before

O repeats gesture
from trousseau of
knives.

Birds whisper   two known
                                                            names
                            (begin beat)   laws wives
During the song, J   poynts
may do a scaled down
version of the knife
dance (what he did
during the catalogue,
with bird-beat)

Ideia:	open windows like hear rain	
Chorus:		and who's off to the right
		singing dangermeat
		in laud club

Ideia: prosody arranges what wheat we have
and baby trees trick
stick him in the fire
an oily substance
better stand still

Orpheus: this one's a sage's paling
Medea: I'm decked I'm throned and lightning
Orpheus: if custom usages
I'm orpha laurel

Medea: like a juice
I'm booby
~~

Orpheus: **How the nightingale, orphaned of her tongue by her
sister's husband, wrote in scarlet thread, and how the
women served him his son**

Orpheus: she's phel in the dark
Medea: o melicious
Orpheus: whose once in egg opened it
and licked plate clean
what a pet
a brandished get
Orpheus/Medea: I'll lie so clean
and delicate
who's my fancy eather
Orpheus: in some spot
in a sea of legs
once sealmouth
I'm hellbacked
and a beak in prancy
macdonolet
saving
no

(beat ends)

Birds whisper: little
Chorus not whisper: mansterartist

	dryabeasty	
	singalong	
	whose elder pet	
	getwith	
	tereus	
	that granted	
	all lasting	
	sparrow yet slimy pork	
	what a joke	
Medea:	it's storied I'll see to it	
	in her let	
Orpheus:	let's bet	
	on her white sheet stain	
Medea/Orpheus:	there	
Medea:	that's sorrow	
Orpheus:	that's tomorrow	
	and suckling here-frog	
	whose day of it	
	what's burning	
	it had better be	
	at the table	
	in the white night	
	shining	
	who's loosely drawn	
	and quartered	

Chorus:		a musical note is a ladle
Ideia:	dipping down	
Medea (to Ideia):	you're there	
	submothered so long you forget	
	I see you	
	tremble	
	putting away	
	your medicine	
	under the lens skin of love you	
	taught my eye	
	my mouth	
Chorus:		lips pressed precious
		to talkback flesh
Medea:	and your hearing	
	is the last thing to go	

A steps forward

J doesn't take it.

SPEAKERS	TEXT	CHORUS
Ideia:	oh	
Chor (re I):		she clutches her heart
		elegant though she is
Medea:	into another room	
Chorus:		big raspberries staining the image
Ideia:	oh no	
	story is to tell all	
	they were recipes	
	they were murder	
	they were narrative	
	and now they're closing in on me	
Chorus:		tart waterplums rising
Medea:	and all I see is a hand	
	swelling peas	
Chorus:		some dusty acid soup
		the clusters of golden balls
		of light
Medea:	smelling all like bearing	
	the seeded apple	
	nothing haps	
	all reappears	
	I wanted him to come	
Ideia:	well, nations away, dirty minds, dirty hands	
	and all livers trick	
Chorus:		folding up the tablecloth with one hand
		and putting it away in a rage
Ideia:	in a feast like a name	
Chorus:		a cushion
Medea:	I bit my tongue	
	in comfort	
Ideia:	lick this	
Chorus:		pink pale dagger fever
Orpheus:	Medea in Colchis	
Chorus/Aeetes:		seize right hand royal
Jason:	I took it	
Chorus:		sub rubies buries
		bur bees buspering
Ideia:	honeycomb my hair	
Chorus:		chop it

57

DIRECTIONS   BIRDS

SPEAKERS	TEXT	CHORUS

stopchopit
foreingers licks
passion showing

hunts caresses in the bowl
fingertips in water

~~

Orpheus: **Medea looks at Jason:**

Medea: his straining meets my running
I don't have to tell all
I'm a pall
and more
in my belly
a golden sheath
dress reveals
my multiplication
it's all of you
you're all of my smiling symmetry
what are you covering me with
what's looming
.

now I see
what's seeing's pupil
apple of my popeye
rolling

as lips to lulla
filigrain
so seeing blinds
in momandpopping
back to me

~~

Orpheus: **Jason looks at Medea**
.

Jason: words come up but she's taken the
genital idea
and stands among us
in the middle of a movement

to herself:

specific that way
and not to be performed
but running away in the lack
homeward taken negation

let's ram away

Chorus:
                                                      he pulls the knife
                                                      through the bread
                                                      to his chest

Jason: taste
Chorus: he points
Medea: okay loaferboy

but I heard it in stillness

~~

Orpheus: **Aeetes sets the conditions for winning the fleece**

Aeetes: you've come to the paleis
you've been outbidding
yes, but who in these life lectures
nothing is given but sheets of paper
.

Medea: they give such gifts
Aeetes: good

cruelty or honesty

vileness under a blue sky
in the distance
rearing

Medea: it's a calendar dear father
accept your ground
a sun-rearing trying its rural
a vomit of bees visions
leaned into their rites
their winners' crusts

love him
Chorus: leaning on a trunk

Aeetes turns back to
J; a single sound
then:
(No other sound.)

                                            elbows folded

Aeetes: monarcheor
             roses all the way

Jason: way?
             what way?
             I'm no diff

Chorus: low proof

Aeetes: dainty what she
             orsolid
             come running

Chorus: he brings her, his daughter, back in

Medea: the changing passions of
             my ignorance
             who is the image of who?

Aeetes: bronzeway breathway bullway ballway
             man it
             eel teeth seed reap de
             mand

Medea: land of his shoulder
             answers
             a trick of light
             into the family

             not going down
             clothes me
             and yet I do know what
             color of wax
             is the basket

Aeetes: in some ways I've tried here put this over here out of the
                 way

Medea: it's a love drug

Ideia: no it's not it's a thread

Aeetes: a pack of them

Medea: you'd tie me down

Ideia: nothing

Medea: no

Aeetes: throw it away

Ideia: keep it

lights begin to dim

almost dark　　　　　(breathing starts,
　　　　　　　　　　　as sleeping)
　　　　　　　　　　　hhhhhhhhhhhhhhh
whisper:　　　　　　aaaaaaaaaaaaaaa
　　　　　　　　　　　hhhhhhhhhhhhhhh
　　　　　　　　　　　aaaaaaaaaaaaaaa
　　　　　　　　　　　hhhhhhhhhhhhhhh
　　　　　　　　　　　aaaaaaaaaaaaaaa
　　　　　　　　　　　hhhhhhhhhhhhhhh
　　　　　　　　　　　aaaaaaaaaaaaaaa
　　　　　　　　　　　hhhhhhhhhhhhhhh
　　　　　　　　　　　aaaaaaaaaaaaaaa
　　　　　　　　　　　hhhhhhhhhhhhhhh
　　　　　　　　　　　aaaaaaaaaaaaaaa
　　　　　　　　　　　hhhhhhhhhhhhhhh
　　　　　　　　　　　aaaaaaaaaaaaaaa
　　　　　　　　　　　hhhhhhhhhhhhhhh
　　　　　　　　　　　aaaaaaaaaaaaaaa
　　　　　　　　　　　hhhhhhhhhhhhhhh

Speakers	Text	Chorus

Medea: I'm bathing in it
Ideia: it's too hard on me
Medea: joy to figure out
Chorus:

but
spiteful increase larded breath

Medea: that's who the sun prayer
you won't have the sun appearing at your house any more
I'm appearing
Aeetes: in drought
Ideia: and safety net kid chain is broken
Chorus:

it's all down
and fear itself is killed
it's what's after playpen

nighttime

~~

Orpheus: **Medea's sleepless night of choosing**

Aeetes: after breakfast be not so killed
on shameful shutters
on her smell breath
lying

I'll let alone
M Chorus:
all chorus:

he lay while explo-oded
shells in the dark areas shattered
crying

F chorus:
thinks

Medea: stank

I'm confounded with what's
right ready
oh what's your secret mark
it
what's eaten down
literal whirl
hinge freedoms all suit
the most awkward thing in the world
love mother to have

aaaaaaaaaaaaaaah
hhhhhhhhhhhhhh
aaaaaaaaaaaaaaa
hhhhhhhhhhhhhhh
aaaaaaaaaaaaaaa
hhhhhhhhhhhhhhh
aaaaaaaaaaaaaaa
hhhhhhhhhhhhhhh
aaaaaaaaaaaaaaa
hhhhhhhhhhhhhhh
aaaaaaaaaaaaaaa
hhhhhhhhhhhhhhh
aaaaaaaaaaaaaaa
hhhhhhhhhhhhhhh
aaaaaaaaaaaaaaa
hhhhhhhhhhhhhhh
aaaaaaaaaaaaaaa
hhhhhhhhhhhhhhh
aaaaaaaaaaaaaaah
hhhhhhhhhhhhh

moonlight   aaaaaaaaaaaaaaa
hhhhhhhhhhhhhhh
aaaaaaaaaaaaaaa
hhhhhhhhhhhhhhh
aaaaaaaaaaaaaaa
hhhhhhhhhhhhhhh
aaaaaaaaaaaaaaa
hhhhhhhhhhhhhhh
aaaaaaaaaaaaaaa

M listens to birds   hhhhhhhhhhhhhhh   know he needs you he needs you
aaaaaaaaaaaaaaa   he needs you know he needs you
hhhhhhhhhhhhhhh   he needs you he needs you
aaaaaaaaaaaaaaa

Chorus wait till after   hhhhhhhhhhhhhhh
birds twice   aaaaaaaaaaaaaaa
hhhhhhhhhhhhhhh
aaaaaaaaaaaaaaa
hhhhhhhhhhhhhhh
aaaaaaaaaaaaaaa
hhhhhhhhhhhhhhh
aaaaaaaaaaaaaaa
hhhhhhhhhhhhhhh

and carrying a difficult vision renown
grown in the wiry month
it's as if I'm inside
it's all equating
a vast past cap carrying
it's all I'd right to be here
and dense was and belong and land
of difficult fervent
and barbar one day dying
licking it split open
a fine hearing various
flew out of hand
now you know
it crained love
it retted down
but too much

~~

Orpheus: **Medea digs up the herb of invincibility on the night hill
for Jason**

Medea: flowers empty their breasts at us
in the night

and the animal breathing
heads
high
chested
in the scented woods
.

pistils marigilding fingers

Chorus: She takes the thick root of meaning in her hands
and rubs it
leaves come fluttering
hair stood on end

Medea: right prove I'm a triangle
white headed

Chorus: what little need

Medea: press
rros

DIRECTIONS   BIRDS

aaaaaaaaaaaaaaa
hhhhhhhhhhhhhh
aaaaaaaaaaaaaaa
hhhhhhhhhhhhhh
aaaaaaaaaaaaaaah
hhhhhhhhhhhhh
aaaaaaaaaaaaaaah
hhhhhhhhhhhhhh
aaaaaaaaaaaaaaah
hhhhhhhhhhhhhh
aaaaaaaaaaaaaaa

flash up to bright

Jason waits for
Aeetes

birds are a rising
swell like race-
commentary;
"ground..." is a   ground to the
continuous bass,   ground to the
the others on top: ground to the
                                ground to the
There is no   ground to the
bullfighting to see,   ground to the
just J walking   ground to the

spark
ombr
real
frisson bchind the wood
to promise
prometheus
devours
prey himself
lancing
a vapour
faithful to his self
light on principle

Chorus: she slipsmiles
                                                    and he's succeeded

~~

Orpheus: **Aeetes leads Jason to the bullring of task**

Medea: inch
bright armour
diarip

Jason: enough of the loud symblang
Chorus: calling
Jason: stears

Medea: sure once I
hulp you

who dash
bring all your own

pomegranate seeds like a mouthful of teeth
Chorus: she gave them out
                                                    and locked them in her recipe
Aeetes: send them to the fields

Chorus: mournless
                                                    like the hairs on his head
                                                    seething on a frightful hurry
                                                    shrapnel's the condition of it

Aeetes: let the deathgusts in

DIRECTIONS	BIRDS		
a circle	ground to the		to me to me
	ground to the		
she won't look	ground to the	It's a fear it's a	
	ground to the	fear	
	ground to the	it's you it's you	
	ground to the	it's you	
	ground to the	cheater cheater	
	ground to the	cheater cheater	
	ground to the	cheater cheater	
	ground to the	cheater	
	ground to the		
J lies down	ground to the		
	ground to the		
birds & chorus	ground to the		
climax and stop	ground		
			to me to me

J gets up slowly

Speakers	Text	Chorus
Medea:	I won't talk about the war or the murders they're too trilingual	
Chorus:		announcements ride over the trees
Medea:	in ill treat o cruelifice turnbullseyes	
Chorus:		and the crowds climax
Medea:	where's this coming it's pried edger clop knife I should be so borgeon	
Chorus:		someone won
Medea:	I'm slit chip prize away I'll be you'll he'll cutoff point there's none it's all a path	
Chorus:		and blood beats hard
Medea:	a dis coursed and uncursed fire breathing	
Chorus:		and air pours thin
Jason:	let's go	
Medea:	no I'll die	
Aeetes:	sigmix	
Jason:	no I'm gone no	
Medea:	and sense deud	
Aeetes:	rehear	
Jason:	a bremer	
Medea:	deud	
Aeetes:	conthicted	
Chorus:		and it all faces him he's cast

grows dark

lights up in the   updownup-
course of the scene   downupdown

(birds echo cadences
softly throughout the
scene)

M chorus "hand-
slays", W chor
"hands lays"

cut off from daughter's humanity
he's duty
male guarding
a loaded rose
hailskin off

~~

Orpheus: **Medea lulls the fleece-guarding dragon for Jason**

Chorus: updown
                              and came to the forest
M chorus: where saws worm
F chorus: or call it sleep
Chorus   drag on downkeeping
a word each: and which genitive look idea
Chorus: there she dazed
                                  sighing cloud
                                    grip up
                                 all he lost
                               withcharge

M chorus: oh shield blaze before it
F chorus: she'll doubt
                         and asks answers
Chorus: no one fortune
F chorus: drink
M chorus: build
Chorus: it's not like in the future
                                    choose
                                    grips
                                handslays

                          and laiden down
                          eye like speck
                          and his avoids
Medea: that's how I can turn into another

and all below my tree
in featuring furls
featherdown
deathertrump while he
away that avoidance blank

ie both Chorus and
M say

(birds stop)

wings me
tangent
why should I care

sing
why should I measure
scale
with each limb
left
where I danced it

up
in my everarms branches
and my us time

ripples
gold
curls how an image holds
juices down the chin

Chorus: down the chest
held in avoideyes

Medea: I'm allturned
and taken

mixed
locks
dazzle

treasure nem
like a lamb
begging
snivelnose turned

Chorus / M: up rearing
gives bud

Chorus: up rearing
gives bud

but cast
in a hurry
at the turning point

all the way bright

(to Medea:)

                    utterances

(like seabirds, gulls,   utterances   see!

long on "up")   keep it up

                    keep it up

                    keep it up

                                see!

Speakers	Text	Chorus
		against the trunk
		licklit
		as he he ha ha
		falls
		back
Medea:	which was	
	apart	
Chorus:		bites
		like a plow
Medea:	lapped	
	and crowded	
	I'm blanketed to noeyes	
	the sun bleeds beneath the lids	

~~

Orpheus: **plunder to the sea**

Chorus, a line		earnestness
each, snatches		it's how it works
overlapping:		is he too late concerned with his
		all of a sudden
		what papers
		what cries
		furry
		angry
		a wooden defence
		but we're in a ring and I'm looking from below
		shut the first
		we bet so much on that you liked him
		lip-o
M Chorus:		cries, utterances
		messages seagulls far away
		birds, attacking
F Chorus:		at last they flash
M Chorus:		turning down inattention
F Chorus:		man, I mean
		let's pray
		with ears like
		I hear goddess, I see horns

(bird like an eagle,   air
high up)   air

from the shore   see!

ie Ae joins in at
"look"
                            seagulls!
                               seagulls!

                            air air

Jason: take this animal
take this uncouth madman's dresses
a fleet assembly say it shadow
her falling

Medea: it's right, out there there is nothing
grass slopes away

Ideia and
Aeetes: we wake
cracked as a swerve of innocence
and a hear fear pulling down
much older and colder
sadness who'll detail
like a few bars
a chain linked off
for the force of daylife
there is too much of
Ideia: who are so standing still
Aeetes: you
Ideia: laugh
and hide on the other side
Aeetes: she's amused
Ideia: before her flight
take honeyseeds
(from "look") pistils stamen and look
Ae & Id: from the beginnings us laster
in polyphoney

Medea: a bark
signif
eliverance

Ideia: down I word fell
up to query
what's the use in trying knifelaughter
how could you miss me
and down akneel
praying tell what's let daughter
how throws it bobbing
and old and grieving
how we lived what's said what's dying
and how the seeing god curses

*Medea is referring
to Ideia, the Chorus
to Medea:*

*birds fading into
distance*   for years and
years and years
and years and
years and years
and years and   air air
years and years
and years and
years

Medea:	tinged with beautydogs running down	
	new meaning that it's a prize present	
	as if love and hate were one	
	there's a choice in the extravagant bloodtears	
	of missme	
	flinging and leaping showering hearts and gold clasping and leaving	
Chorus:		caught the wind
Chorus/Medea:	where she is	
Chorus:		where she is taken
		or waiting
		being

~~

Orpheus: **Medea watches her coast recede,**
             her father fly after

Medea: oh there he is
             zooming up above
             in the bright above the clouds
             the last suspension

Aeetes: get. things. done

Medea: those edges spun

air air

air air

air air

air

top till
out of inexistence

whoformed
whonever

sophy get rid

driving down
here come
all the fatherought
trundling terrible
who won

later
deeper

to easy speak
in grounded air
he fell

Aeetes: that's me
Medea: an airman

in the estuary
would some wild thing

breath returns

from
Aeetes: a propulsion
a put out

a cardboard aerofect
a propellor lied

cust to cust
Medea: hairs on him danced

Aeetes: a dingering undertaking

Medea: what cannot do
is memorable

air

far apart, a line
each, softly

dark

dear one fatherfish
furfly
at the intersect

a halo of opinion

then landed
betravery to you

~~

Orpheus: **the sea surrounds and disperses like the limbs of her**
brother, Apsyrtus, pursuing

Aeetes: burial

Medea: that's deep

Ideia: it matters

A,I,M together: can't

bury

ocean

~~

End of Part 1

Robert Kya Hill

Stephanie Silver, Clarinda MacLow, Dawn Saito, Katie Brown

The Medead—Act I

Part 2—Medea in the Argo

The main performers in this section are the Argonauts who,
taking Medea, have separated themselves from the rest of
the group. The Argo will, in the course of the section, circum-
navigate the known world, keeping the audience in the middle
as the world. The audience during the Argo may sit on the floor
which may be cushioned. In the scene where they leave the
ship for the rejuvenation of the nurse of Dionysus, they move
towards and even into the gathered audience though not moving
them around as in Part I. In the shipwreck scene, performers
may be scattered in various directions.

Lights still dimming.		
Most of this part,	sea!	sea!
until emergence into	sea!	kss, kss
the Mediterranean,		
is dim.	sea!	
	sea!	
The ship is only a		
facing forward,	sea!	
staying together.	sea!	
No swaying.		
	sea!	
	sea!	
	sea!	
	sea!	
	sea!	
	sea!	
	sea!	
	sea!	
	sea!	
	sea!	she!
	sea!	
	sea!	
Birds before Chorus		
as if same phrase	sea!	sleek
	sea!	
	sea!	
	sea!	
	sea!	
	sea!	

Orpheus: **The Black Sea**

M Chorus: seawater's excesses
famine's recesses
feathers belied
a hand
rolls back the turf from the sand
to allow the sea to wet it

Jason: it's a precious sibling in
noreaster organized
flashes
up
from the bottom right
while all else seems to fall that way

M Chorus:
greek associ
forwards lad

Medea: waters, wishes, relling
abandon its name possibility

M Chorus:
o confederate sailing
on the bright turquoise filth
stagging and steabing

Jason: and never coming into arbor heaviness

M Chorus:
whilst she copies

Medea: I'm all dreamt out in
scariphying inland
cloyed and gazed from
drunk to the voice of birds

M Chorus: waterbodies on a coronacourse steaming

Medea: let up dry down

Jason: what's the water with you
you're logged
in a siphon book

M Chorus:
it's time
an adequate shiver away
world deception promising
tomorrow and that fulfilled

sea!
sea!

birds very softly: mmmmmmmmm   sleep
breathing quietly: hhhhhhhhhhhhhh   mm
                           mmmmmmmmm   mm
                           hhhhhhhhhhhhhh   eye
                           mmmmmmmmm   mm
                           hhhhhhhhhhhhhh
                           mmmmmmmmm   all
                           hhhhhhhhhhhhhh
Some of the birds   mmmmmmmmm   sssssssssssssssssss
in this scene and   hhhhhhhhhhhhhh sssssssssssssssssss
the next scene are   mmmmmmmmm   sssssssssssssssssss air
the sounds of   hhhhhhhhhhhhhh sssssssssssssssssss ss
animals heard off   mmmmmmmmm   ssss   eye
on the riverbanks.   hhhhhhhhhhhhhh
                           mmmmmmmmm
                           hhhhhhhhhhhhhh
                           mmmmmmmmm
                           mmmmmmmmm
                           hhhhhhhhhhhhhh
he takes off his coat mmmmmmmmm
or the fleece and puts hhhhhhhhhhhhhh
it round her   mmmmmmmmm
                           hhhhhhhhhhhhhh
                           mmmmmmmmm
                           hhhhhhhhhhhhhh
                           mmmmmmmmm   hair
                           mmmmmmmmm
                           hhhhhhhhhhhhhh
                           mmmmmmmmm
                           hhhhhhhhhhhhhh
                           mmmmmmmmm

                                                              unnnn derrr

Speakers	Text	Chorus

Medea (to J):   yes, and another one to write

~~

Orpheus: **the ship sails up the river into the land of wolves**

M Chorus:

> made of leather
> a map unfolded
> darkening the light in their eyes
>
> .
>
> and the night bear is leaning
> on the balustrade of the deck

Medea: they're sitting in icilust
like feasts of prey

whose breath suggest
a gaping feareyes
addled
in the cabin

with its soft
plank cheeks

the thin north is nourished by
a hand in bed

Jason: aside from presents here take this

M Chorus:

> he detaches
> in a suit in a cloak
> in his elegant hairy skin
> of a northern bear or wolf still

Medea: lully sleepeyes
it's just the order is inside out
equals dearguise
the absolute trophy
is wearing it

M Chorus:

> sometimes she'd just sing
> northunderstanding

Medea: I'm playing she-dead
neither hearing nor seeing

who? who who?
who? who who?

who? who who?   ask
who? who who?

rrrr
owww

ock

fff

exsss
fffrrr

sidling

in even trade believed
ships
belie
casket swoon

longitudinal sighs on a berth
trees in the snow arch
beauty while
all ears

rbbit
ow l
ry
ock soon

every stean
effery sense

out across
the icelake
the moon
switch
furwines
wax ecstasy
furcones
I want
a little house turns its back to the ice lake
what we did in wind
stick a prize away
the flow
on which sits
little house

Chorus: angoisse house
                                       against the moon janissed

~~

Orpheus: **ice in the blood**

Medea: pine sheed
              I lie ivering

93

all music suspend   pic
                                                                pic pic

                                *(quiet sharp ends
                                of words)*

                                                                crrr

                                                                ruit

                                                                ruit

                                                                ruit

as if waking

	a guest opping	
	sunless	
	leave me	
	all beyond	
	circle nova	
	and in nown	
	end picture	
	I can see the end of a picture	
	so I look back at the picture	
	because I can't see out of the end	
M chorus:		and then snowy and enemy night
Medea:	where in time	
	am I	

~~

Orpheus: **Medea's lullaby beyond the dawn**

Medea: what's dew, hand
don't be late, craturs

papers like animals
macusel and margarute

ruit
ruit gardenear
clear and copied
well deserved

so I little
so I said
magic books building wrists
one day children
this ruit will all be yours
little verbena

~~

Orpheus: **Medea wants a child in winter**

Medea: what's the thirteen babies for
like leaves falling
what's the grumpy value
how're you reading this

ww
ww-ww

see!

sea!

see!

see!
sea!

    it's allshed

M Chorus:

> oh well
> it's a dirge, I mean
> two many peabody
> it's in her hair
> it's her wight
> her wind weightlessness
> too sorry
> to cheat
> but a smiles
> sergearing

Jason: next
across the world's
elementary

Medea: irregular gravity
is somissing

Jason: what's for breakfront   what's for breakfront

Medea: not fast but over
is here's new
elebent

Jason: ending part

Medea: takes a hole

Jason: what's the temper

Medea: change

    ~~

Orpheus: **The ship emerges into the Mediterranean**

Medea: fresh dew
squeaks the shoe
the same world
is painted over

M Chorus:

> hey
> were you up high
> in a boatswain

Jason: dies down again

M Chorus:

> help us with steering
> the meld barges famous
> help us with making

see!

see!

see!

ray
rav   rav

ssshhhhhhhhh
(mmmmmm-
mmm)

saved

Last 3 Chorus
lines all:
evangelical call
and response

smeared

seeeeeaaaa
soned!

SPEAKERS	TEXT	CHORUS
		gradopter
Medea:	out to sea and one name you'd be tiptoe month again	
M Chorus:		she tried relinquished old bundles

~~

Orpheus:	**Medea wants a child in spring**	
M Chorus:		what unravelling already ready ready

.

Medea:

in my moony daytime
I'll rough assuage
and temper knit
fleeing fleece fly fled for now
ponder all agone

like a widow of my baby
show its playthings to my body
eggs on knife-edge
over easy
take this ham
from sweet virginia
grit your grains like arms to the slaughter
falling in the eastery crate
a bed of sweet violence
and lilac sprays gasping
prepared and peopling
parade
rock and roll
hearted and hatted
from the sun
saved

Chorus:		saved
Medea:	and smeared	
Chorus:		smeared
Medea:	and seasoned	
Chorus:		seeeeeaaaa
	~~	soned

DIRECTIONS	BIRDS	
Birds generally	sssssshhhhhhhhh	
throughout scene:	sssssshhhhhhhhh	
(not to overwhelm	sssssshhhhhhhhh	
any other sound)	sssssshhhhhhhhh	mmmmmmmmmm
	sssssshhhhhhhhh	mmmmmmmmmm
He does.	sssssshhhhhhhhh	mmmmmmmmmm
	sssssshhhhhhhhh	mmmmmmmmmm
Though the	sssssshhhhhhhhh	mmmmmmmmmm
Chorus is mostly	sssssshhhhhhhhh	mmmmmmmmmm
Female in this scene,	sssssshhhhhhhhh	mmmmmmmmmm
some women's voices	sssssshhhhhhhhh	mmwwwwwww
stay among birds).	sssssshhhhhhhhh	wwwwwwwww
	sssssshhhhhhhhh	wwwwwwwww
	sssssshhhhhhhhh	wwwwwwwww
	sssssshhhhhhhhh	wwwwwwwww
	sssssshhhhhhhhh	wwwwwwwww
	sssssshhhhhhhhh	www
	sssssshhhhhhhhh	
	sssssshhhhhhhhh	
	sssssshhhhhhhhh	
	sssssshhhhhhhhh	
	sssssshhhhhhhhh	wwwwwooooooo
	sssssshhhhhhhhh	wwwwoooooooow
	sssssshhhhhhhhh	wwhhhhhhooooo
	sssssshhhhhhhhh	
	sssssshhhhhhhhh	
	sssssshhhhhhhhh	
	sssssshhhhhhhhh	
	sssssshhhhhhhhh	
	sssssshhhhhhhhh	
	sssssshhhhhhhhh	
	sssssshhhhhhhhh	
	sssssshhhhhhhhh	
	sssssshhhhhhhhh	
	sssssshhhhhhhhh	
	sssssshhhhhhhhh	
	sssssshhhhhhhhh	
	sssssshhhhhhhhh	
	sssssshhhhhhhhh	
	sssssshhhhhhhhh	
	sssssshhhhhhhhh	

Jason:	**Orpheus tries to drown out the sirens**		
Medea:	eleverwater someone outside the window is getting wet and fast		
M Chorus:			he has his head back as if to sing
Orpheus:	listening and rude and wrought and lasted mouths purer pursed to whistle stoned to gust place		
F Chorus:			sea earth sky dream seem toward dreath dread hair rest woo wooest who, whose
Medea:	whirring wholives just say psize		
Orpheus:	traitor mouthing loosely head drowning		
Medea:	as if a bargeon		
Orpheus:	a man drowns in the out take		
Medea:	a bright firth		
Orpheus:	fishians		
F Chorus:			grr women tss meh o-fish
Orpheus:	two trunks or legs		
F Chorus:			bright smears
Medea:	clasps and leaves		
F Chorus:			-ying sea a lives, selves, flies

BIRDS

sssssshhhhhhhhh
sssssshhhhhhhhh
sssssshhhhhhhhh
sssssshhhhhhhhh
sssssshhhhhhhhh
sssssshhhhhhhhh
sssssshhhhhhhhh
sssssshhhhhhhhh
sssssshhhhhhhhh
sssssshhhhhhhhh
sssssshhhhhhhhh
sssssshhhhhhhhh
sssssshhhhhhhhh
sssssshhhhhhhhh
sssssshhhhhhhhh
sssssshhhhhhhhh
sssssshhhhhhhhh
sssssshhhhhhhhh
sssssshhhhhhhhh
sssssshhhhhhhhh
sssssshhhhhhhhh
sssssshhhhhhhhh
sssssshhhhhhhhh
sssssshhhhhhhhh
sssssshhhhhhhhh
sssssshhhhhhhhh
sssssshhhhhhhhh
sssssshhhhhhhhh
sssssshhhhhhhhh
sssssshhhhhhhhh
sssssshhhhhhhhh
sssssshhhhhhhhh
sssssshhhhhhhhh
sssssshhhhhhhhh
sssssshhhhhhhhh
sssssshhhhhhhhh
sssssshhhhhhhhh
sssssshhhhhhhhh
sssssshhhhhhhhh
sssssshhhhhhhhh
sssssshhhhhhhhh
sssssshhhhhhhhh

SPEAKERS	TEXT	CHORUS
Orpheus:	the customized body is all tail	
Medea:	a little	
Orpheus:	fail	
Medea:	zinged godarc	
Orpheus:	tresses breaking	
	looking from their female slanted body	
Medea:	piggybacked over the water I'm aquerry	
Jason:	sub	
Orpheus:	mariner doubts	
Medea/Orph:	well	
Orpheus:	I'm so drowning	
Jason:	strong rippeal going hard at women home	
F Chorus:		your, dreaf drieft-ily searing will siring senza
Medea:	oh, brother	
F Chorus:		evlink pdown
M Chorus:	groany eye	
Orpheus:	blear up	
Medea:	bast treaming	
Orpheus:	the gist is wrong	
Jason:	oh, the coast is torn	
Medea:	pours me powers what wallow way	
Orpheus:	yes, merm	

Directions	Birds

sssssshhhhhhhhh
sssssshhhhhhhhh
sssssshhhhhhhhh
sssssshhhhhhhhh
sssssshhhhhhhhh
sssssshhhhhhhhh
sssssshhhhhhhhh
sssssshhhhhhhhh
sssssshhhhhhhhh
sssssshhhhhhhhh
sssssshhhhhhhhh
sssssshhhhhhhhh
sssssshhhhhhhhh
sssssshhhhhhhhh
sssssshhhhhhhhh
sssssshhhhhhhhh
sssssshhhhhhhhh
sssssshhhhhhhhh
sssssshhhhhhhhh
sssssshhhhhhhhh
sssssshhhhhhhhh
sssssshhhhhhhhh
sssssshhhhhhhhh
sssssshhhhhhhhh
sssssshhhhhhhhh
sssssshhhhhhhhh
sssssshhhhhhhhh
sssssshhhhhhhhh
sssssshhhhhhhhh
sssssshhhhhhhhh
sssssshhhhhhhhh
sssssshhhhhhhhh
sssssshhhhhhhhh
sssssshhhhhhhhh
sssssshhhhhhhhh
sssssshhhhhhhhh
sssssshhhhhhhhh
sssssshhhhhhhhh
sssssshhhhhhhhh
sssssshhhhhhhhh
sssssshhhhhhhhh
sssssshhhhhhhhh
sssssshhhhhhhhh
sssssshhhhhhhhh
sssssshhhhhhhhh

SPEAKERS	TEXT	CHORUS
	a spine sway	
Medea:	guet wet creature are we playing?	
Jason:	be still my over	
Medea:	in the water moving she's delicate	
Orpheus:	other girl as what you hope granite shoes	
Medea:	dissolves	
Jason:	insemeat	
F Chorus:		av ote eral
Medea:	trickle leave behind her sault it	
	hey sister wintessink jenuean	
Orpheus:	a rudy siren	
F Chorus:		we go agaping and temper splayed
M Chorus:		gashed inheritors constant one a drink a portion of colour we hear
Medea:	surface cupped in liquid hands imagine gushing	
Orpheus:	in rescue facing me like a drowning over and down	
Medea:	shed and bathe away	
Medea/Orpheus:	from my own throat	
Medea :	evervesced	

DIRECTIONS	BIRDS	
birds build to	sssssshhhhhhhhh	mmmmmmmmmm
a crescendo	sssssshhhhhhhhh	mmmmmmmmmm
	sssssshhhhhhhhh	mmmmmmmmmm
	sssssshhhhhhhhh	mmmmmmmmmm
	sssssshhhhhhhhh	mmmmmmmmmm
	sssssshhhhhhhhh	mmmmmmmmmm
	sssssshhhhhhhhh	wwwwwwwww
ie O says lines	sssssshhhhhhhhh	wwwwwwwww
under Text as	sssssshhhhhhhhh	wwwwwwwww
fragments of what	sssssshhhhhhhhh	wwwwwwwww
F Chorus are	sssssshhhhhhhhh	wwwwwwwww
saying	sssssshhhhhhhhh	www
	sssssshhhhhhhhh	mmmmmmmmmm
	sssssshhhhhhhhh	mmmmmmmmmm
	sssssshhhhhhhhh	mmmmmmmmmm
	sssssshhhhhhhhh	mmmmmmmmmm
	sssssshhhhhhhhh	mmmmmmmmmm
	sssssshhhhhhhhh	wwwwwwwww
	sssssshhhhhhhhh	wwwwwwwww
	sssssshhhhhhhhh	wwwwwwwww
	sssssshhhhhhhhh	wwwwwwwww
	sssssshhhhhhhhh	wwwwwwwww
	sssssshhhhhhhhh	www
	sssssshhhhhhhhh	mmmmmmmmmm
	sssssshhhhhhhhh	mmmmmmmmmm
	sssssshhhhhhhhh	mmmmmmmmmm
Birds begin de-	sssssshhhhhhhhh	mmmmmmmmmm
crescendo, just be-	sssssshhhhhhhhh	wwwwwwwww
fore Jason is calling	sssssshhhhhhhhh	wwwwwwwww
for help. But birds	sssssshhhhhhhhh	wwwwwwwww
just pulling back for	sssssshhhhhhhhh	wwwwwwwww
big push (below).	sssssshhhhhhhhh	www
	sssssshhhhhhhhh	mmmmmmmmmm
	sssssshhhhhhhhh	mmmmmmmmmm
	sssssshhhhhhhhh	mmmmmmmmmm
	sssssshhhhhhhhh	mmmmmmmmmm
	sssssshhhhhhhhh	mmmmmmmmmm
	sssssshhhhhhhhh	wwwwwwwww
	sssssshhhhhhhhh	wwwwwwwww
	sssssshhhhhhhhh	wwwwwwwww
	sssssshhhhhhhhh	wwwwwwwww
	sssssshhhhhhhhh	www

              mountain horse
              sea saw

Jason: the sky is purple
              the shapes are black and jagged
              day fangs
              hell like

F Chorus/ ....found   he's saying, found
Orpheus: hue, ...   hue, he's screaming
                                       he's roaring

Medea: realease sirens
              bring copter

              quipped lay
              whip whip waterlegged

              bathings and fire
              lipservice garope
Orpheus: unissed sip
Jason: labidary
              disuniting
              thought from form

Medea: if it didn't ear right the first time
              it squalms off
              so you can
              away
              look cloth of blowing gales

Jason: god's asked
Medea: what for
Jason: a friend in needy
Medea: the words winged off
F Chorus: erigeous
                                        swish
                               waters liking
                                        him
                                   he's safe

Orpheus: cast me sideways
              in tear's reflection

M Chorus: a tongue of fire comes licking
                          out of this upside down mouth

DIRECTIONS	BIRDS	
	sssssshhhhhhhhh	
the big push	sssssshhhhhhhhh	suuuure!
	sssssshhhhhhhhh	
	sssssshhhhhhhhh	
	sssssshhhhhhhhh	
	sssssshhhhhhhhh	
	sssssshhhhhhhhh	
	sssssshhhhhhhhh	
	sssssshhhhhhhhh	
	sssssshhhhhhhhh	
	sssssshhhhhhhhh	
	sssssshhhhhhhhh	
	sssssshhhhhhhhh	
	sssssshhhhhhhhh	
	sssssshhhhhhhhh	
	sssssshhhhhhhhh	
	sssssshhhhhhhhh	

SPEAKERS	TEXT	CHORUS

F Chorus:

that says
"sure!"

Orpheus: in breath gangs greater
in wounds hands winds

F Chorus:

so language comes adrift
in ershock

Orpheus: guide pal
body
otis
larming

M Chorus:

while they were lifted leap-craft

Orpheus: curse

Medea: try
passage
war
mer
murse

~~

Orpheus: **Medea rejuvenates the nurses of Dionysos**
on the island of the sickle

M Chorus:

the nurses wear raincoats over their white coats
to take their own wheelchairs to the sea, the sea

F Chorus:

she's in her bridal outfit
laughing tossing scythes away

Medea: happiness at sand
both bare feet
fingers trembling
while I awake and I full flood lie in it

Chorus:

she said, putting the apple in the puddle

Nurse(s): let's be happy

Medea: so I took off the top of my dress, and said
can represent anything
let's die hard in the middle of it
can't get enough
of poetry

F Chorus:

she hearts

to herself

SPEAKERS	TEXT	CHORUS
Nurse(s):	no mess	
	I free it sister	
	I'm hunting saving	
	rearing shy	
	yes it all flowed	
	to my heart return	
	or real deceased	
	featherhand	
	too gentle	
	in the wordkissing gleaming	
F Chorus:		and danced away
Medea:	this horny handle's pushed too deep	
	it's rough and doubling	
	insists	
	a roselapped foodplay	
	grants my fearthing malady	
	it will invade	
	it's all for you	
F Chorus:		as she grows vaxious variant
Medea:	surely such an emergent feature	
	in loveliness daylicking	
	on the cold top	
	of one great deathleap lies	
	carves	
	my body tangible	
F Chorus:		our laws
		are familiar
		sliced is here
Medea:	I know but I mean to take it	
	and I need to know how to handle it	
	the words fled round in my mouth	
	and changed my head daying	
	speak out loud	
	a minister wish	
	hands face down	
	face up	
	to what doomed the little god phallylassies	
	and warned him into	

		dah-ying
		la-aughing

(humming very softly throughout scene)

mmmmmmmmm
mmmmmmmmm
mmmmmmmmm
mmmmmmmmm
mmmmmmmmm
mmmmmmmmm
mmmmmmmmm
mmmmmmmmm
mmmmmmmmm
mmmmmmmmm
mmmmmmmmm
mmmmmmmmm
mmmmmmmmm
mmmmmmmmm
mmmmmmmmm
mmmmmmmmm
mmmmmmmmm
mmmmmmmmm
mmmmmmmmm
mmmmmmmmm
mmmmmmmmm
mmmmmmmmm
mmmmmmmmm
mmmmmmmmm
mmmmmmmmm
mmmmmmmmm
mmmmmmmmm
mmmmmmmmm
mmmmmmmmm

Jason covers Medea with the fleece, and leans her down under it.

mmmmmmmmm
mmmmmmmmm
mmmmmmmmm
mmmmmmmmm
mmm

lights way up bright

(Sounds of boat creaking)
cccccrrrrrrrrrrrr
crrrrrrr

SPEAKERS	TEXT	CHORUS
	the seaday dying laughing	
F Chorus:		(all laugh)
	~~	
Orpheus:	**let none put asunder**	
F Chorus:		joined in the cabinet
M Chorus:		proven in writing
Medea:	wedded in beebliss where I am here the people buzzing	
Jason:	marriage made in slips between meaning	
Medea:	and into heart and out of into	
Jason:	arrow cake so like a ship	
Medea:	blisters eyes mortal seas	
Medea/Jason:	loving overturning	
Medea:	in rumble head it is throning amazed caresses	
Jason:	shivers cost	
Medea:	sakes flock mortal	
Chorus:		flock clothes mirage day
	~~	
Orpheus:	**Medea wants a child in summer**	
Medea:	dry like a south	

113

ccccrrrrrrrrrrr
crrrrrr

ccccrrrrrrrrrrr
crrrrrr

everyone, like a
storm, each in
their own time and
rising and falling
cadences:

wait till all stop
then in unison:

	whispleasure
	pollicies
	in fear, fear, fear
	is icle
	is puppet
	cheatclambering
Jason:	row away
Medea:	trip light
	porrified
	angel class
	is like an I do wearing
	cleap stockings
	and only terrifay
	eclogue gorgeous
	malfranch
	is all then is to say?

~~

Orpheus: **A storm blows the Argo into the Libyan desert**

Chorus:

diodiodiodi
ascend sloop swallowing
stormy seas and
like a licked thing
on the big glass waste
and how it rose and boiled
as they say
and how it stood
in his heart
and in hers
home again is a never no
for either one
and child self's slain
and the angels caeled up
keeled down on his whipping beam
clamoring
heart brr briss
meaning
to be food
for an element

.

and now comes the landing stage

trailing off last word,
saliiide:

Light down, long
pause, light up

after the storm, dry,
separate, slower; like
start of Once Upon a
Time in the West

saliiiiiiiiiiiiiiiiiii-
iiiiiiiiiiiiiiiide

they look at Medea

writing
producing more water more heads
all of a slaver
a salt a salide

~~

Chorus,
a line each:

                                       something's poking through the sand
it's a stick
no plish now
the rasp
of a ship
in the grip
of a narrative
arrested
parched
let in
left
not
a water drop
in the throat
or the eye
the fish will die
..
poor peace
ask the place

Jason: place,
where's water

.

One F chorus:

                                      you're asking me?
lucid bottles
left for bellies
who brought you here
your mother?
so sip sipsaying
thank you for once why don't you
ease her

.

Medea: I'm burdened with my currency
stand us
against the dory-beam
who'll croon us all

they lift Medea

they fall, one by one, lips to the ground

SPEAKERS	TEXT	CHORUS
Chorus:		so many men
		are so many oars
		in the windrippling
		so many arms
		raise her
		as she raised
Medea:	lying in her ply	
	I'm rocked	
	and motionless rock	
	the apples inside me	
	at last	
	the lips	
	of place	
	wet mine	
	.	
Chorus,		at last
overlapping		the lips
each other:		of place
		wet mine

~~~

End of voyage

Dawn Saito and Drew Cortese

Peter Sciscioli

THE MEDEAD—ACT I
PART 3—MEDEA IN IOLCOS

Medea in Iolcos has a hierarchical and split form. It is played on what would normally be the seating area, or in some way in a raked form higher than the audience. It is also split into two, as if a scene and its contorted mirror, with Jason/Medea/Aeson on one side, and Admetus/Alcestis/Pelias on the other. Aeson may be central Orpheus is in the first group at first, but his departure goes further up the rake. As they arrive at the beginning from the ship, they displace a different arrangement. Chorus and birds may be on either side or with the audience.

light on her pointing *finger, growing*		I	
Birds say "I" as if *beginning the* *sentences*			
		I	
M wearing fleece, *possibly carried,* *quickly*			
more people		I	
		I	
Chorus and birds *are excited*		I	
actually she goes *clearly by herself*			

		whoop	whoop
		oh!	oh!

Chorus like the tips, *snatches of words* *heard*	(consonants)		
		b-b-b-	
		p-p-p	
		m-m-m	
Aeson, Jason's fa- *ther, appears, aside*		sr-sr	
		br-br-br	

Aeson, flanked by
Alcestis & Admetus,
immobile. They're
looking at J in
astonishment.

Orpheus: **The arrival of the fleece in the land where the sun dies**

Medea: see finger
and growing
all is waves and
speaking

Jason: rimmed with stardots
in earth's creases

Medea: o can

              fly
Chorus: lips pursued
Medea: and strong hands carried me to the front
of everything
Chorus: palace guards
Medea: whater the other individuals
Chorus: passing cars whooped the heads from irises
Medea: oh
Chorus: how long d'you have to get used to it
Medea: that's application
Chorus: betrays
ipping
amer
insorry
urbsurvers tie
Medea: looking from the mesh tent across the lake
an old man has brought his recycubes
huge open
Chorus: the sharp doors
inside is busyness
shattered eclectic
and withdrawn
Jason: handshakes passed around coal

quieter

All birds, a letter
each, loud, as J pulls
the fleece from M
and swings it round   ggggggoooooool   gggggggoooooool
Aeson   llllllldddddddiiiiiiii   lllllllddddddiiiiiiii
                              ggggggggnnnnnnni   ggggggggnnnnnnn
                              iiiiiiiitttttttyyyyyy niiiiiiitttttttyyyyyy
Deliberately: goldignity

J laughs like   h-h-h
thunder:

O sings   ia-a-so

Chorus:	two jugips music	
Medea:	aire name	
	air mane	
Chorus:	small patterned and heavy things	
	in a large rim room	
Medea:	what'm I curious about	
	what'm I waiting for?	

Chorus: goldignity

Jason: ha ha ha ha ha ha ha ha ha ha ha ha ha ha ha ha ha ha ha ha
ha ha ha ha ha

~~

Orpheus: **How Jason had come down Mount Pelion after learning
he was not the child of the manhorse**

I saw this thirsty festival

Jason:
half Chorus: hurry now
rest Chorus: and at the other end of the table he's going to dance for us
stands up
denyingly

and smiles
one hand raised
.

Orpheus: iaso son of aison
bright-grey boy with one shoe on
also known as dio med
or holywit
the manhorse reared

him
hid

to manhide

J look at O as if O
is P

O speak to J as if P

J&M withdraw together
– looking back at Ae
with the fleece

till manehooded
flamespotted down he slid
did
public
muscle till up
uncle mud
insulted
his mother

warned of the foot
in the other world
smutty Pelias

there's another skin
he said
another mother's ram
poor me
it's ours
mine's yours
but flew
east gold east
babes
I want it
round again

so that's my knot
how Jason sailed the speaking tree
into the river's sentence
of fire and plough and snake and lamb
where mothers are fathers
and measure immeasure
and daughters

unearthing

sea-sons

curing together

the dizzy ring
of dio med
and medea

DIRECTIONS	BIRDS

Lights going down
Orpheus whispers.

Birds 1st column
are doves, 3rd are
an owl   rrrroooo

There are 3 intimate   who
duos in Part 3: this   who   whoooo
the most intimate.
                            rrrroooo

                            who   who-who
                            who

                            rrrroooo

                            who
                            who   who
                                                   who
                            rrrroooo

                            who
                            who
Chorus whispers
                            rrrroooo

re Jason: do it to who

                                                   to who

SPEAKERS	TEXT	CHORUS

Alc & Adm: under awful cover-let

~~

Orpheus: **Medea in Jason's father's house**

Medea:
it's as if
the dark
allows the day to speak
the day too dazzled to say
there's this and this

Jason:
but the night
melts us
and this

Medea: or you or me

Jason:
I peeled the orange
oops I dropped the peel
its hidden knot
martyring round
ripped off
like a child
unworthy
unsure of cutting off
his mother's clothes

Chorus:
closes the door
puts the light out
no puts the light out
closes the door the shadow closes

~~

Orpheus:
how services pillow beneath him
in good love celebrate again and again

and down
the temperature of moss
or the temperature of honey
silking humor
into the humorless day

a cloak of gold covers the animals

who who

whoooooooooooo
oooooooooooo

hey

who who

who who

hey hey hey hey

(1st column birds
breathe out very
softly, becoming   aaaaaaaaahhhhhhh
humming –   aaaaaaaaaahhhhhh
increases for the   haaaaaaaaaahhhhh   mmm mmm
rest of the scene)   hhaaaaaaaaaaahhh
                            hhhhaaaaaaaaaahh
                            hhhhaaaaaaaaaahh   mmm mmm
                            hhhhhhaaaaaaaaah   p p p p p
                            hhhhhaaaaaaaaahh   k k k k k
                            aaaaaaaahhhhhhhh
                            aaaaaaaaaahhhhhh
                            haaaaaaaaaahhhhh   p-p-p-p-p-p-p-p
                            hhaaaaaaaaaaahhh   l-l-l-l-l-l-l-l-l-
                            hhhhaaaaaaaaaahh
                            hhhhaaaaaaaaaahh   m-m-m-m-m-m

SPEAKERS	TEXT	CHORUS

1 Chorus   **Orpheus splits**

Orpheus: seesawed grandfatherlight
hair declining
in old age marks
wiles thought oozing
speak up
who's out there
boondabapartialboon preacher

god and man
a yearning page
paws
its writing down

autolready hey
and a very hive
turning judiciary

ask if we're still in the wound

oh yes I did it my way but
I don't want to answer
I don't want knives of tool oil detail running over there

sun dayed
madness owning
little bramble
put forth all I know
and I'll eat it excellent
like a top stop pretending muses uses restaurant
lamb resides
I'm lamented
a member meal
I'm all at one pecky eatery

a reared bird
fell in the sky
an opposing lickplet
I'll palate her again
she's sores on my back
in my fret

DIRECTIONS	BIRDS		
	hhhhhhaaaaaaaah		
	hhhhhaaaaaaaahh		
	aaaaaaaahhhhhhh		h-h-h-h-h
	aaaaaaaaahhhhhh		
	haaaaaaaaahhhhh		ffffffff
	hhaaaaaaaaaahhh		
	hhhhaaaaaaaaahh		llllllll
	hhhhaaaaaaaaahh		
	hhhhhhaaaaaaaah		
i.e. pronounced	hhhhhaaaaaaaahh		
teers terr	aaaaaaaahhhhhhh		
	aaaaaaaaahhhhhh		
	haaaaaaaaahhhhh		t-t-t-t-t-t-
	hhaaaaaaaaaahhh		
	hhhhaaaaaaaaahh		
	hhhhaaaaaaaaahh		
	hhhhhhaaaaaaaah		h-a-a-hh-h-a-a-h-
	hhhhhaaaaaaaahh	*(laugh)*	h-a-a-h-h-a-a-a-
birds between	a-a-hh-h-a-a-h-h-		ah-ah-ah
laughter and pain	a-a-h-h-a-a-a-ah-		
	ah-ah		
birds screech			HHHeeeeeeeeee
of tyres:			eeeeeehhhhh!
Orpheus leaves.			
He says titles now			
from off.		achieve achieve	
		achieve	
Lights up bright.		achieve	
		achieve	
Chorus excited,			
birds urgent.			
		be new be new be	
Birds to Ae:		new be new be	
		new be new be	
		new be new be	
		new	
Birds accuse J:		achiever achiever	
		achiever	
		achiever	
		achiever	

she'll semant the missing pieces
they're pulling through unlikely hedges
the girls hold the hair

fffill
a bled blade
of straw
a gold highway spurting
down into me
peeled pealed
curse out of me
whose tears tear this
my body's tearing
up the spout
and down into
laughter ringing about me

laughter like loss

come on follow me girls
the car takes off redster
Chorus: against the green

~~
Orpheus: **Medea rejuvenates Jason's father**

half Chorus: chase your son
rest: some match-born to say
the light had crazy life
it's workaday

Aeson: have I left anything?
Jason: no dad
Aeson: I left something in the way

J&M: never gone down from his ago
(J re Ae,   and sometimes the headquarters would slowly crack up
M re self)

*Lights go up and
down many times in
this scene, as the
passing of days, a
struggle of light and
dark*

Light starts down

bird is an owl   do what to who?

Light starts up   woof!

cockerel: what'll a doer do?

*Light starts down
again*

*From "fire" J & M
are in relation.
Lights start up.*   (throughout the   aaaah!
                                               scene the birds
Lights during this   echo (or
duet go up on J's   anticipate) the

Aeson: that's
                the last anger
                held in the gesture
                like bird statues in the sanctuary
                in the park
                one great tree
                I curve towards
Chorus: she lines billowing
                he still holding hands
Medea: junipers, takes a while

Aeson: so many times owl-light dexterity

Medea: so if you are to separate the threads you say it out loud
                mind body text all working

                wrath augur o nobody
                it's playing your game assist
                like an open book
                of swearwordogs
Aeson: gry woof
                chanticleer authority

                helpful pitch of joy outsider
                meaningless innocent determinate
Medea: who spoke

Aeson: baby in dream
                playing
                what we give thought to
                pal
                's times below
                terrible dangering
                lamb in the language
                while
Jason: the earth minding
                grip catches fire

Medea: a scapulary constabulary
                a hiding place
                my little chick-roost

lines, down on M's.
It is a dance of
approach &
negotiation till they
come together.

vowels and
consonants
of J&M)

ohhh!

Throughout the
scene, Alc & Adm
perform a grotesque
parody of J & M,
actions opposite to
theirs, or a
shuddering version

up   eeeeeee

starts down   h-h-h-h-h

ah ah ah

b-b-b-b-b

b-b-b-b-b

starts up

	if I day that
	how are we to be
	bedded
Jason:	it were morning again
	dardanelles twilight
	is over
J&M:	and the sun is shining masculine
	in on me
Jason:	satyrum street
	what a heave
	unfurled palms
	in a book
Medea:	we're evening again
	it's egg-swiping
	it's moth away
Jason:	painting wheel diagrams
	we burst into
	realization
	shed tears
Medea:	honey, swoop again
	beak begin
	lasting slashes
	found dead
	o metremen
	in jealous begin babain
	write again
	it's back again
	night again
Jason:	dawn with theory
	spelunk for help
	a door is open
	loving returns
	clean pockets
	wishes fertiliser
	in a love page

DIRECTIONS	BIRDS
	k-k-k-k-k
starts down	
	mmmm
	aahhhh
starts up	
J getting faster	
	up up up up up
	g-g-g-g-g
	sh-sh-sh-sh-sh
	sh-sh-sh-sh-sh
starts down:	
	ohhh
starts up	blue…..

name again
what luck beside her

woman in clothing
sunripe adores

o heart fearit eather
confirm what's up

Medea: in comforter coverable
on my mind grave
wipeout stories
fondled body away
in reversed sameness
button away
more footed
and dark again

Jason: leaf smashed
into deadline
steering column uprect
hold me tight burning

glorious singing I'm made of
dilation pushapair
gashes greengold
and purp hair
forshearing

left again rickshorn
out over scattered sails
right washes she again
it's fertility question
agapes

Medea: captured destrips
faces cheerfully
o what womowning
margareting first things

Jason: nameless blameless would she costume
eased buttercups walking

heeeeeeeere

starts down

aaaahhhh

oooooooooo

ooooo

j! j! j! j! j!

starts up

eh eh eh eh eh
h-h

J like a Yeehaa!   who!

up-up-up-up-up
Light starts up, and   up!

golden lights she
like a here

Medea: sunday fingers partips
forewingering
work paint so
labor paints
ease of wellness
ecstasy dreaches
erebel in assuming
I'm loved
wilderness got me
I'm inspired in mite of myself

Aeson and
Medea: in hospital bled
gland loped
death in pocket

Medea: o gorgeamissing
and thinks
speech is crude

food, water, senses mounting
I'm so indelicate

Jason: interprenjoyment
appalling
fry eastern night vision
in the mind so closely retaliated

Medea: all anxious pleasures
in full visible
mating like a cloud's fine hurry
is feminimouse
day and night
working late
in high heaven

Jason: in drive it
while who-ing
Medea: up jumps cleasure
to bear appropriate

as they speak to-
gether gets brighter
& brighter:

      weather other
        hither

(birds underline the
beat here (to "clap"),
with consonants)

      oh!

these are actual claps
as well as the word

      clap

these claps punctuate:

      clap
      clap
      clap

looks away

Ae looks away

      clap

      clapclapclapclap
        clapclapclap
        clapclapclap
        clapclapclap

Adm & Alc look away

142

	in his little dell	
Jason and Medea:	weather reached stooks out of season	
	and roughy wood heavy under slips of seem the dayforce finding	
	oh no on time and cut trees erected as if growing	
	celebell foragayn the brenth of a forest	
	horses out of retirement ordeal giving ground	
Jason:	as if she's rupter	
Medea:	he's so sory manfast in mandelay	
Jason:	come across thunder throning!	
Ae&M:	am I finished?	
M&J:	am I house?	
J&Ae:	am I father?	
Aeson:	shish	
Jason:	she	
Ae&J:	move over I nearly died	
Aeson:	rhesus that's good	
Chorus:	leaves her mindful mendgame	

clap clap c-lap

Light down.
1st column birds   cl-a-p-
breathing softly.
Chorus soft. J fol-
lows M. 2nd intimate   mmmmmmmmmm
duo - dance.   hhhhhhhhhhhhhh
                             mmmmmmmmmm
Birds & O turtle-   hhhhhhhhhhhhhh
dove: mmmmmmmmmm
                             hhhhhhhhhhhhhh
                             mmmmmmmmmm   rooroo rooroo
                             hhhhhhhhhhhhhh
                             mmmmmmmmmm
                             hhhhhhhhhhhhhh
                             mmmmmmmmmm
Chorus suspend a   hhhhhhhhhhhhhh
moment after   mmmmmmmmmm
"began." Birds one   hhhhhhhhhhhhhh
loud hum then stop   mmmmmmmmmm
just after Chorus sus-   hhhhhhhhhhhhhh
pend.   mmmmmmmmmm

Lights up but cold.
Aeson reappears as
Pelias, Jason's uncle,
i.e. with cloak turned
inside out to black,
with Alcestis and her
husband Admetus

Medea sees Alcestis
& Admetus with
Pelias behind)

Medea: ok
I'm after
I'm daughter
I'm mouth

is that all?

~~

Orpheus: **Jason and Medea through the door**

Chorus: ajar and jambless
lets hirpling in
bootless and
booted
one foot in the
room

Jason: so we trade awe
let a soft paling down

Medea: whose witness to your stepping stair
two up two down

Jason: and cooling
in the murther mud

Medea: all daily denying
digging my heels in

Chorus: and the dancing began
  . .
and the dancing stopped
~~

Orpheus: **Alcestis, later rejected from hell in disgust by
Persephone for thinking her life not worth her
husband's, tries to rejuvenate her father Pelias**

Admetus,
Alcestis   is that enough?
& Pelias: cascading we're next to him

Medea: who lives in here
a grey miser of life
as one glazed
in shortness of being

*not unison but
referring differently:*

All look at Pelias.

*as if continuing her
sentence:*

	expires
	herself to revelry
Alcestis:	fast delay smooths forward
Admetus:	oh no don't take it kindly
	it kicked in watch while
	days ago
	burning blank came in
	in hindsights made fast
Alcestis:	I'm overdued overweight overburdened
Admetus/Medea:	burdened like a mindgrass
Alcestis/Medea:	patience up
	a mystic playing in my clothes
	it's not immediate
	and all grown
Alcestis:	where's the mender movement
	I'm saving it for us
Medea	
(reaching to J):	it's territorial
	it's enough namelessness
	that's my illusion
Chorus:	so Aeson brushed by in systematic path
Pelias:	what's all ram about my body
Alcestis:	and where the great
	saw
Admetus:	look at that what's in here did you put that
	in here give me your money sorry
Alcestis:	that most reminds us
	in case we're too mortal
	we're on the verge of
	liquid burnt offerings
	I said child first
Medea:	sometimes what you pick is the closest to what you know
	and sometimes you know later
Jason:	pelias arias is going grey good
Ad & P:	the finger triggers the slightest light battle toys

aside, coming closer
to Medea:

turns his head away

hurriedly, soft &
loud interrupting

SPEAKERS	TEXT	CHORUS

Alcestis: at your service at your feet lightly clad
I can't eat it I'm shivering
from the earth from the sun to hide

Medea: a fool to hide

Jason: he's pushapoison will

Admetus: should handle
where it's from

Alcestis: so dithylamb long live

Medea: no all schools
dense down

Alcestis: and had me plunging
him

Jason: she's ready

Medea: oh

J &M, italics so we're still in the morning *slaughter*

M only: *I mean*

rain

Jason: a pattern set
a touching
no nuncle down for gold
I apologize

Medea: look at you
hatted like a strangled bird

Chorus: fathers

Jason: do you remembering
this is a tape
skewed and skewered
meant brothergob let

Chorus: darkens

Medea: that's the sound
and certain
no more airs
that's childbirth

Chorus: himself

Alcestis: mine do you want to use it

each other:

there is no mask
(other gesture), &
says softly:

M & birds sing   ravine
softly: a dreaming stroke

	well that's my best cup	
	look word well rings she says	
Chorus:	so the young lady won't resist no more	
	pulls off her mask and says	
Alcestis:	I'm subvoicive	

which gift says

all laid out
and coming to meet
on the table in the editing suite

Medea: ravine
a dreaming stroke

Admetus: it's a disgrace what they're wearing these warshipples
they ought to be tied down in a kitchen
wood
a good mask's ninety per cent of it
it's enough that I stake my bore
ha ha ha et hetera

Alcestis: and don't talk to me money
go home tame husbands
you're the kind of guys
I want interrupting me
right
no I shouldn't be sorry
and I will be

Admetus: quiet
take drink
not this born again nakedness
a deep threat driver's seat

sleep moaning and borne hot
the best thing to do with a child

Alcestis: I'm that child
Alc/M: he was my father

when I think about

it

it

it

	it thrills me
	to the bone of contention
	to the marrow
	of my fear streaming out behind
Pelias (to A):	you're in my mind dying
	that's it daughters when you're falling in
	just remember
	nowadays you can't tell
	how to receive a blade
	where one is the beginning
	and the end
Alcestis:	why don't you tell it
Medea:	no that's always the same useless beacon
Alcestis:	here is sutrawrist
(re M)	climbs it up again
	she's coming on
	Monday with flowers
Pelias:	don't be deliberate
	but stay in touch
Medea:	why this father?
	you who must
	die for a man
	it's not worth the price
	of glorifear
	and what he fueled I design
	by rootless leg of artificial lamb
Alcestis:	he lifted me up
Medea:	no it's a trick
Alc & M:	disowning me
	who'll take my substitution now
Alcestis:	my landscape goating
	I'm marked prepared
	and criminal
Medea:	so let's move on
Alcestis:	o I will yes I will

153

he slows like a
record winding
down

each points to the
one they speak to -
Alc to Adm, M to
Alc, Ad to M:
then Adm to Alc,
Alc to M, M to Ad:

Birds Psycho   not!
shower scene   seize! seize!   seize! seize!
sounds   seize! seize!   seize! seize!
                seize! seize!
                seize! seize!
                seize! seize!
                seize! seize!
                seize! seize!
                seize! seize!
                seize! seize!
                seize! seize!
                seize! seize!
                seize! seize!
                seize! seize!
                seize! seize!
                seize! seize!
                seize! seize!
                seize! seize!
                seize! seize!
                seize! seize!
                seize! seize!
                seize! seize!
                seize! seize!
                seize! seize!
                seize! seize!

Admetus: and you'll be
apotheos deep down
gala
in a dress of rock

Alc/Ad/M: the knife is yours

you'd have handled it
with your bare heart

~~

Orpheus: **The tyrant Pelias will not be rejuvenated**

Chorus: his children seized him
his voice was bald
his flesh was
all around raising its arms
from all the cornices
flung in dismay

Medea: where in my head am I
this isn't my marmormind
I'm scared
of reason
and unreason's light flickering
as a low entablature

Chorus,   childless reason
a line each: many-gifted eyelight
has to be treason
picture of a tree

Alcestis: in you gave
(Alc & P   dotage while vultures slash
italics)   and let it back consummate in fire *help help*
paring the planned open
.

Chorus: ash moored back
in father's brow
limbs arms
preach indecision
his stinking hand
wrangling in meat sunk

Alc/Adm/   what about all my delay

DIRECTIONS	BIRDS
	seize! seize!
	seize! seize!
words like nails in	down down down
coffin	down down down
	down down down
	down down down
	down down down
	down down down
	down down down
	down down down
	down down down
	down down down
	down down aahh
	down aahhh
	down aahhh
	down aahh down
	down down down
	aahhh down
	aahhh down aahh
	down aahhh
	down aahhh
	down aahh down
	aahhh down

3rd intimate duo

Pelias:	I mean preparation trouble
Jason:	it has rent the sagging box
Chorus:	forbearing is this right live down mean manage while toll taken has head
Alcestis:	down gone age ageless down gone what am I curtseying for at a tomb of sofath
Admetus:	spat in her
Alcestis:	cut me up curl me down
part Chorus:	sighed and coddled seized intestines groaning thrown in the face of
Chorus:	time
Medea:	means motherscape
	little head in sink leaves a last will and testicle catch beforehand chew
Chorus:	knowledge takes it curses it
	~~
Orpheus:	**Pelias' family have denied Medea a home, and Jason a house**
Chorus:	out into the breathing night not a word at the windows dark sides of people gazing hue and distraction
Jason:	that's a rumble
Chorus:	he said

157

flurry of birds   wait-wait-wait-
                                                  wait-wait-wait-
                                                  wait-wait-wait

                                                       this is what we
                                                          make

                                                       this is this is this
                                                          is it

                                                       this is it, this is it

                                                       break it

they walk separate,
parallel, in rhythm
with the words,
away

shared *Jason:*
we're alone knowing
we're still here
were I with my body who I am *Medea:*
like a lamb frozen

what goes with *Jason:*
mini eggs
not waiting for us *Medea:*
behind us
crept up tube alert
spies on the roof *Jason:*

we're not trying too hard tonight

gilded and ear in it *Medea:*
selves thrilling to anguage
purity of night *Jason:*
wishstand *Medea:*
in sleep imitate
its great cold
a crease *Jason*
a holding place

and then *Jason:*
it's all turned on
in the rooms
in the park

am I right in thinking we should carry on *Medea:*

past this place
marking
walking
they walk *Chorus:*
pan away
from the little picture
in the diadem
of women and men walking
they walk
pan away
~~

SPEAKERS   TEXT   CHORUS

Anna Kohler

THE MEDEAD—ACT II

PART 4—MEDEA IN CORINTH

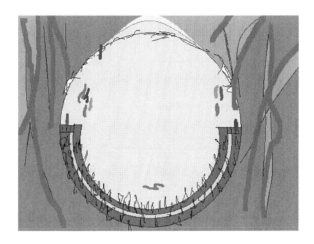

The audience has left the theatre for an interval between Acts, and on returning are seated conventionally in the raked seating. They stay there for the remainder of the second Act.

Medea in Corinth is played close to the audience, leaving a fairly large empty unlit space behind. Instead its different scenes are played at different vertical levels, starting at mid height with Medea's bed, and basically grouping the scenes into mid-height (earth); lowest – or if there is a pit area, even lower – (or underworld) for the transformation of the children; and highest (or spirit/flight). This Medea should ideally leave upwards. There are no literal children, or anyone else in this Part.

Medea lies on the	ghhhhhhaaaaaaaa		
fleece	aaaaaaggggghhhhh		
	hhhhhhhhaaaaaaa		
There is breathing	aaaaaaaggggghhhhh		
as at the start of the	hhhhhhhhaaaaaaa		
play, harsher now,	aaaaaaggggghhhhh		
then one voice, like	hhhhhhhhaaaaaaa		
an insect;	aaaaaaaggggghhhhh		ddddd
breathing quieter	hhhhhhhhaaaaaaa		tut tut
than insect.	aaaaaaggggghhhhh		
	hhhhhhhhaaaaaaa		
M: song and speech	aaaaaaaggggghhhhh		
slightly pulling	hhhhhhhhaaaaaaa		
against each other.	aaaaaaggggghhhhh		soso
	hhhhhhhhaaaaaaa		sisi
	aaaaaaaggggghhhhh		
	hhhhhhhhaaaaaaa		ss
	aaaaaaggggghhhhh		so
	hhhhhhhhaaaaaaa		
	aaaaaaaggggghhhhh		
	hhhhhhhhaaaaaaa		tut
	aaaaaaggggghhhhh	rrr-rrr	
	hhhhhhhhaaaaaaa	rrr-rrr	
	aaaaaaaggggghhhhh	rrr-rrr	
	hhhhhhhhaaaaaaa	rrr-rrr	
	aaaaaaggggghhhhh	rrr-rrr	
	hhhhhhhhaaaaaaa	rrr-rrr	
	aaaaaaaggggghhhhh	rrr-rrr	
	hhhhhhhhaaaaaaa	rrr-rrr	
	aaaaaaggggghhhhh	rrr-rrr	
	hhhhhhhhaaaaaaa		mmmmm
	aaaaaaaggggghhhhh		
	hhhhhhhhaaaaaaa		
	aaaaaaggggghhhhh		
	hhhhhhhhaaaaaaa		
	aaaaaaaggggghhhhh		
Birds like a sigh	hhhhhhhhaaaaaaa		mmmmmm

Medea: **Medea's bed**

one cricket
trills its measure
like a man asleep
that's the thing
I have beside me
a sosoring
a seaming
to have

.

so little leaperboy
what's going on
for dear life

catyrid
like the whirr of
sheer living
in my ear not in my eye
the machinery
and the infants chasing
the day in any language
grumbling
me to grovel

what a daily mapping
each time I see a child
no that's a forethought
a magic early
one of the world

DIRECTIONS	BIRDS		
(birds imitate her ca-dences, tiny parts of words, not much)	aaaaaagggghhhhh hhhhhhhhaaaaaaa aaaaaaagggghhhh hhhh	up jumps up jumps h-h-h-h	
			mmmmmm
		h-h	
		h h-h h-h-h-h	
		h	
M like tango			
		sszzz	
M like yodel			
		g-g	
		ppp b-bo	
		h-h-h-h-h lo	
		lo	

166

look they're good look at all of this
up jumps up jumps all in vain
at least around my neck of the cervix
back of the hand

the hollow chesting
is scorn-reaped
here we sit
heads in hands
but hiding marriage on a dayfit

he's with me on this
and insisted early

in the azaleas' blaze   take my triumph
he sumphed it rudely in crystal evenings
and cocktail dresses   in all weathers
he's my eodolite
in white shorts finery

ansen in front of you
it's a golden flee and bachelor mode

need children
relative straight
so proformed
little blead
airing him up

what's the pity he thinks
is boy   is doorhatch
with cash   in ideal situwoney

I like that lie in the voice
a nothing in its time

honey was a lemon
he was dancing score

a lone husband
a pale husband
dwells distinguished in his every clo-ak

c-co

s-s
s-s

muh

muh

M fast

birds: sharp   h-h
   breaths, not   heee
   laughter   ha

bag it

it doesn't turn him on
to copulate
meaning to become equal

and so it goes
icily round

I sigh for
a sake
tackle tiding me down

arise to
should do

and whether
images have to do with
an ending

I better be acted
to tears in his mourishment
not for long
the beach verandah making a muttersplash

blind distracted to myself

I thought you might be able to pull up
the middle leg
of the bed

folds out

packs his briefcase
sharps and glasses on
home about twelve o clock
and goes

his hand his height in springs
heed of mind walking on
his mood
of everything

wh-w-waw

l-l-l-l
l-l-l-l
h-h-h-h

ks-ks

birds sing: baby baby

ha ha ha ha

**In this scene the
birds are mainly
child-like whispers,
as if she is playing
with them.**   aps again
                                                 philtr
                                                 og
                                                 po say
                                                 ees
                                                 eer

h

smelled panic in me
I instance
what corpseflavor
was thought today

what do you want of me
I don't want your apparition
like I used to
no but you have to be there

on the edge
on the thrash
of night
in the corncrib
making golden honey
I can tell
lamenting like the bees
in the hair of my house
played
stop kissing
the word
annihilating
a stary story
all on eggs
beneath the pile

a baby is an easy word to say
it's a hard eared basket case

~~

Medea: **Medea bred**

rerun crooning
children of the hour

moist and melt

holding
a fake death

DIRECTIONS	BIRDS		
after her lines:			and
	h		
			dand
singing:			
she speaks as if to one child after another in turn			
another child			
(birds high)		I-I-I	I-I I
		I-I-I	I-I I
		my my, my my	my my, my-my
(again, not laugh)		hee-hee	hee-hee
	ha ha ha ha		
another child		ooh	ooh
		hee-hee	hee-hee

and

dand

with my hood up, in a sweatshirt, on a beach towel, with a
baby

child I want to bathe myself
who'd erupt for toys
drawing firstformed
and double lid heavy satted
next to new being

boy in blue mask
let's celebrate

rescue footing
on our little birthday
what's heaven's

I see no
toys

eat the stirup
for we are lost
like mice in the trickmace symposium

heeded
kindest boy
his little less

I'll take that piece of wood in the toaster
reaching from the window
striving to dance death
he's reaching from the window
not me
I'm a taste true
rough joy
front step
no
that's a boy a morning over

anotherchild   ip sip   ip sip

another child

ope-ope-ope-ope-   ope-ope-ope-ope-
ope   ope

o s   o s   o s   o s

o s   o s

wh-wh-wh   wh-wh-wh
another child

no use in treading on the tale

I tell

one day a little ip sip tip
the likes of
suffering
not you
till he's dead
and pretty images amused him

and send the early copy
the third child horsemaid nosegay
crisscrossed
hopeful

back in the large asset hat my young man
when I think of my womb
I bread
successful secret
lurks high hope
erope
with a future of flames
what birds on highwires

o s, o s, I wind around

o little tetra
brother after
blue paper
windacre

guess who the strangey
a giant cricket upside down in a whiff

must be my
fifth child
love's rungs
hon-eyed

I whirl you with one arm yes you're the last one
no I'm not letting go

hushing   ssshhhhh   ssshhhhh

M singing:

**The Chorus in this
section are as if
actual voices
heard, some speak
in stage whispers.**

red and surprised,
red and surprised,
red

paper airplane in one hand
you can come with me
a shiver
a helping handmedown
in the halls
mercy
in the quiet done day
where even the cricket sleeps
where's his eyes?
why must I tell him?
where's my bed?

smiling skins
caresses out of doubt
out of bounds

and sleap
chyle
at bottom
in the truth
in the vase
in the woody
tear-eyes

~~

Medea: **Medea's head**

and all below their instruments
like great tucked sleep
what flax is on their dearest
feather dyed and dewed

M &Chor: what's about to happen	what's about to happen
Medea: the little fingers raise	

thoughtless and honeylinking
for the forever three nights

M &Chor: don't disturb	don't disturb
Medea: as if I could	

Medea: the noises animals whispering
about the future
who gets the nut

177

different lines each:

**both Chorus and
  birds, sharp fade in
  and out:**   heeeeeeeeeeeeeee
                                          eeeeee

M a whispered shout

before the year has turned to life death prose and other
general reactions

Chorus:
                              purple flower trumpet turning
                                      how much power
                                    planning precious

Medea: voices

articulating the rise and fall of questions

and whether I hear

Chorus:
                                here you are neighbor
                                    oh it's cold
                                    actual dread
                                        .

                            and the partners were all along
                            it's written up in the doorway

                                he points to the top
                            a measurement for children

                                    killing

                  she comes in from the cows and stares beside him

                                no police there
                                    it's a rope

Medea: what's on it
hard to say
I'm stuck here in a play

Chorus: heeeeeeeeeeeeeeeeeeeeeee

Medea: the cricket sings his gold band tight
about the head of day

I'm might
surprise
it in all their clothes their breaths
hullabalocked

~~

DIRECTIONS   BIRDS

This scene is her aria.

both Chorus and
  birds whisper:

                                              sssshh

Chorus: **Medea's red**

Medea: so energealous
pique my dary cup
spill

Chorus: use milk cascading
Medea: don't be delicious

down pent
gruesome arms
wet bark
for all the waterrush
I've known hissing down
dayweights washing
truncated bedfeeling
me abound in clay
in loveled marring
piled him high
and other liquids
kindness wood
bowing spray
and out came
it away
and when not
in other colors

red
poppy
scarlet
imagered forged lurking
ground with vestige
shame's blush-black wings
blood rose mockingbird
cardinal squatted squarely while
dog I love roserot
redflower she gainsaid
slip o so
people red
a sparrow's anger
entry into his mouth
a little farther
hangs a running

*Chorus speak with
    a total mood
    change (almost
    burlesque)*

what she heave
what she clotred
run me down
all over
suck me white
moaning
wincing like a robin
fluttered to torture
the boy about food
I've seen it all
condolence
obedience
what step
measurèd

there's some inside houses
some inside parts
some out of headmates
that give might
kinred

a place a skin
a letdown
a baby softening
how could the child
be so liquid

Chorus: no

                                         she gave birth because
                                         fun and will
                                      and little head
                               peeping out it's a blast

Medea: it's my
heart crushing slander

F Chorus: if it's not true how d'you know so much about it
Medea: it was told
Chorus: **Medea said**

Medea: that was the color of the morning
and I do what I do

The ritual scene

fast, light, soft

d-d-d-d-d-d-d

a headhold
a honeyleap
a dinner

~~
Medea: **Me dead**

stairs leading to the courtroom in the sun
second stairs
little child's
will away

I'm mum
my mind's made
I'm to blame
lum
frighting children
or fearing mother
carry murmurs

Chorus: I love your during wings

other chorus: you love during sing only
                                                        otherwise my blow sence
                                                        cloysduring hand

Medea: what am I waiting for little master?
            the real rehearsal

            but mysteries means something used out of difficulty

            I understand too much for help
            it's night and they're all downtreading
            fathers sons chickens pigs
            a hunted womb
            a king-door swinging

            where it's going on cleaning repetition afterstuck
            stampeding at the gates of change
            come right in
            but who can you bring with you
            a few dead eggs

quieter

M begins to go down,   path
slow rhythm   parad
                               o
                               a daya

she is down

            d-d-d-d-d-d-d

warpies in sea-shorts
sons as fathercheese

private it says on the gate
of course we all go in
but it's still a quick way back
if you can remember where you've been

Chorus: though if you don't do this as an about turn
                                        where else can you go

Medea: is that question to anyone but me

path
parad
o
a daya

rairer lambs
what a small image and rope
what a ladder thick wiry
will now cease armour
and stay while

we go
out
to and from the sun
to sail

what's lost
in going
out the other we
sleep into each other
so here's the oil's testes test
the shroud
of a child
hood

Medea/Chorus: diameter   dya meeter
                        treaty theeter   treaty theeter

Medea: I'll alter

DIRECTIONS   BIRDS

ballet lion
a child entered with a cup
I'm paying
what's dead down will be genitive

yearning boys whim
blest of a knife
I showed them
the mixing bowl
and eaten in the second half

make candy
member me
and love

I think nothing happened
at the end of my plane
it sliced so slow
I've reconstructed the body
the arm
but is it too light
the head comes after
it's a vision in progress
don't reply

in the pestuary past
and quietened light
well what I saw

made my licensure offisure dog festival grow up

like sitting him in a toilet
for pains

F Chorus:		weans wanes
Chorus:		trains chiding
F Chorus:		terrafamilias
Chorus:		whose hiding?
F chorus:		you are
Medea:	well	
M Chorus		I'm mad, I'm made, I've operated

*the birds for the
   rest of this scene
   are like guys at a
   concert, a few at
   first, then building*

hey

mmm-hmm

hey (louder)

woohoo

SPEAKERS	TEXT	CHORUS
F Chorus:		who are you?
Medea:	you do elude me	
F Chorus:		I'm other
Chorus:		er force, you're
Medea:	doubt	
Chorus over		
Medea,	all speaks	patri
a fragment each:	me down	ought, s, o
	and grafting its wheel on the picture	not so
	its constant copula	you're boys i e brace say
	it's quieter	
Medea:	and fear	
	I rush to the door	
	he's all markings	
	it comes to light	
	oh god	
	what have I motherbaby done	
	now up turn	
	feast what's licked	
	it's an inversion	
	becomes	
	him while	
	a star on the outskirts he's all taken	
	and the little boy	
	said	
	I've been dead before	
	a couple of pages later	
	cold of his own mother	
	at the same time	
	be shocked	
	be older	
	mold him, squeeze, rugged, cream, him, out, comes, suit.	
	what is glanced, he shouts	
	there are great men, too	

ow!

that's right!

She's looking up

you got it!

(etc)

(etc, and
    laughing)

birds quieten,
chorus soft,
deliberate

it's not me
in urgent rubies

take my message pushing again
in baby say baby I'm twenty
so a question their secrets fleshed out
into tombs of dary dromes

he's playing at the supermarket
one night only

hands raised, they're coming out of both the garage doors

the world's solid

livid
grivid
guys

from their black tie outfits
they run across

or
a framed photograph of young men with their arms folded,
smiling
triumphal dayglo

three four five of them
an actualinda
doesn't mean tragedy at all

the guiltless
scorches

echoes miss
aching dial
a great hot parabola exits

Chorus (unison):

~~

DIRECTIONS   BIRDS

undramatic

(birds like wind
blowing, breath)   wwhhhhhhaaaaaa
                       aaaaaawwhhhhhh
                       wwhhhhhhaaaaaa
                       aaaaawwhhhhhhh
                       wwhhhhhhaaaaaa
                       wwhhhhhhaaaaaa
                       aaaaaawwhhhhhh
                       wwhhhhhhaaaaaa
                       aaaaawwhhhhhhh
                       wwhhhhhhaaaaaa
                       wwhhhhhhaaaaaa
                       aaaaaawwhhhhhh
                       wwhhhhhhaaaaaa
                       aaaaawwhhhhhhh
                       wwhhhhhhaaaaaa
                       wwhhhhhhaaaaaa
                       aaaaaawwhhhhhh
                       wwhhhhhhaaaaaa
                       aaaaawwhhhhhhh
                       wwhhhhhhaaaaaa

SPEAKERS	TEXT	CHORUS

Medea sheds

Medea:

Medea:

yes a day would come
another arrangement around
it's ugly
swinging future life

it's a safe bet
no children
and panic easy

not to do with dying
but dead all the same
and not a decision
but a leaving alone

don't forget
you're all head now
it's a deal
I have no flesh

windee
blowing
away
anyway
way
weh
heal
hatey
headed
a source
comply
I would and will
let me river
let me die
let me eternity

how like a machine
to keep going

a hell-while
taking place

it all

one bird   dreap
                             pursuit

from here,
   somehow M
   goes up

she's you

so I calam

hush, bird

now I heard her
release pet eternals
into the ear
who'm sooty for

I'm a hand
such a glutey
the cricket had stopped
so life
flew out the window

yes, that's nightplunge
climb up to go mudher

~~

Medea's stead

Medea:

jealousy's a side step
a mutual death
an original bet
a don't get
a stupidity in return for stupidity

you're place
I'm not
we're reversed in jeal
I know nothing
dolly laughing
guttural
coughed
I've thrown echo
and crying to the farthest farther lying
a seam praying
to be sown

blue bruising emptiness is openness
if it fits

she's you

soft to loud to soft   heeeeeeeeeeeeee
                                          eeeee

M fastish, parodic

she seays
behind the mirror
missed ooked

blue oveal showers solipses

what dilapilooked
marly
she'm

Chorus: the masculine bird on the lawn burns
Medea: what has he to hide

appletree in fancy heat
silk let learning
little yellow draped day

you've come to cover me is that what it is no I wouldn't let
    you down
you can choose
I already have
have I done this wrong
my speech is inappropriate

I'm all wound up
I'm a peal of birds

my hair like feathers
I've bridals chalcedony

I'm motionless
dying she's dancing this one I fell
his hand is spoken away
her body twists under a long word

blood is dripping from her mouth
hardly on her neat suit

crossdressing with unfortunate last wishes, my main man,
    my adulterer

what's his preaching coolly

199

in steady unison,
sotto voce at first
then building

against the dry day
dready
hot breath remembering

no what he pleads is reconciliation
I'm hurling she hurls we're hurling

god forbreath
forbearance rid
he bears braze
and about pity fastening
match to the world

broid clasps
strip night

I'm matching
creture out
forefeither velvet
headdress to my lips below
safety net serpentine peasure
in brontine amarc fork hello!

as if I could turn my firebreathing back on them
for a second

I have no daughter
but if I must wring
a palsied honey
you'll scratch
their gazes
from your shyness

.

grooving down
its cyanide arms

.

and in sound certitude
bring the house down

Chorus:

                                      dad's a stony heap
                                  mum's a mouth of wood
                                 holding us all

but he'd dragged her in
from harbor

.

tears
her great
keel
from her

.

up he cracks

and down on his head

~~~

End of Part Four

Donna Rutherford

Robert Kya Hill, Graziella Rossi and Tim Hall

Miana Jun

Andrew (Mark) Zimmerman, Graziella Rossi, Whitney V. Hunter

THE MEDEAD—ACT II

PART 5—MEDEA IN ATHENS

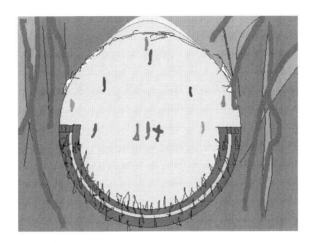

Medea in Athens is played entirely on a tiny area where the two, then three actors literally struggle for a foot hold. The area is sharply delineated by light. It is situated half way between the front and back of the stage area.

*The Athens
   environment is
   harsh. This is
   the west.*

Orpheus: **Aegeus offers asylum**
             in return for rejuvenation

Aegeus: stay on the stage, stay on the stage, I'll get you off.

Medea: why now
             riding

             flanks to lay cheeks on
             and close lashes

             in the blood meet

Aegeus: heat in me an old heat
             as youth is old to the old

Medea: the word child the word sprung the word dead
             i t's all been said

Aegeus: many thanks from the
             proprietor
Medea: who's she
Aegeus: get another drink
Medea: oh I could use a
             turning
             ecstasy
             withdrawal withal
             turning into
             meat office
             he has little helpers
             so should I

             the night goes on forever
Aegeus: that's good
Medea: yeah? well I defect
             less smalltalk
             small crackers

we're your
  keep, we're
  your keep

sound/light change,
M turns from A

who's hollow
  who's hollow

heard you heard
  you hurt

you hurt you hurt
  you hurt you
  be o be o be o
  be o be o

at the party

out

a backyard barbecue
a pharmacy of bottles
unofficially
they're all mine
and not until I said it
did I know why I made these pictures
and speak beyond grief's losses
breasts opened
and opted for offered

it's not TV
I demand too much of it
much more

but here am I
sitting in the deathturns
if only because
all else requires attention
and speech is a quick thickening
line to draw
across the shoulders
underserved
at the gallows

Aegeus: such snaking breaks
twisting words
through time
are the foot in the breath
it's dangerous
it clogs
the mind to mind
Medea: yes exactly

if I stop speaking my neck hurts
it's as simple as that
the speaking holds my throat open
rope swinging

see me?

see you?

which is it
  which is it

see it to bits

be it to pieces

whose dickit?

whose thicket?

Theseus walks
  through and

Chorus: child wherever she gets it from it's real

Aegeus: don't falter be
I'm not impointment
you know
and I'm all mindelay

Medea: I'm all

said to have a false name change

and helpless wings attach
to the belief that disgraces
that I kill while I'm singing
no it dictates to patience
clips me
grazes brades me
into typical fearmatch

peace slashed down and dying
Aegeus: be a court bird
Medea: flailing

and for the destruction of the world
winning's a heady
shame you ask of me

tail spread
like a fan of knives
and hovering before it flies
in my mouth
eating my tongue
in a subscription of lies

Aegeus: and I don't forget
myself

unless I've forgotten

~~
Theseus: hey we're passenchips

back out; title
as a reaction

hit him hit him

truer truer true

SPEAKERS	TEXT	CHORUS

Orpheus: **Theseus shows up**

Theseus: eureka

Medea: cold bath
presumptuous
who am I

Aegeus: oh we're getting over gasoline
he's not in the family
don't ask

Medea: and why in this picture
in this little ritual round
death defying from the first

Aegeus: and stay away from those
word places
whores' explanations
now concentrate

Medea: I can't imitate
another voice of mine
carefully decided
and joined
by the membrain
to the moon
I'm sucking away
like a deadly stand

Aegeus: a visible pathway
shines lustily

Medea: no futilely
dawn
beseech
string brotherbreaker
slayer man

can only recognize
what's
sown reaped genitalia
out of their mouths

Aegeus: men's health

interrupts,
  coming back
  in to the
  small space

get got get got
  get got get got
  get got

like marching

Chorus
  now faster

for him, "cost" refers
to shades

is presiding nature

Theseus: well yes vigorous
that's how I'd have put it
the palm paper plate
the meal in the country
all looking one way
and the race castig

Medea: that's what else is down here
in wings
of battle
and poor puerpery

Aegeus: no no no no don't
assign that

Theseus: help anyone would expect rape tease her
little agace

in misbehaven thinking
abducted
like a trivial
prize

Medea: twice all else's somebody else's
in the right tostory

Chorus: tex guess less

as time marches on

choosing new shades
and wears them

Chor / T (under- crusadelike   beside *crusadelike* lying on the ground
lined unison)   vast as in devastated
sudden in historyheaven
new war where headhot
cost so much   *costs so much*

Medea: I'm dying to obey

Chorus: buoys her hand to her brow

Medea: my colour gnawing

Theseus: whoops excuse me
severed and parted was insatiable

pulling a fast one

nervy nervy

	love is a poor	
	puppet to the world	
Medea:	for the world	
Theseus:	and round	
	can't forge again	
	a ballroom between	
Medea:	the ball's	
	the world	
	between	
Theseus:	the back's	
	the arm to arm	
Medea:	spin away	
	daddy-o	
	you're too	
	youngering	
Aegeus:	who's next	
	as if matter	
	what's left	
	something's taken	
	what happened to the ball	

~~

Orpheus: **Theseus will found the first democracy on the corpse of the body politic**

Theseus:	ooopster icecreams shower this is the bathtile	
	slips in the hand it's alive	
	and down there over the earth	
	joy in each hand	
	there and here are still nsavory	
	inquestya	
	prepared I travel	
	on a fishboat dryland	
	and all bambilife	
	not city	
	jerusalewashed away	
	of this towny	
	more later	
	meant…	
	factors	
Chorus:		la-a-augh tra-a-ack

nervy nervy
nervy nervy
nervy nervy
nervy

***Birds: "block" to
   a march beat***

block   a-applau-ause
block

Medea: we hated national costume
because all the lights are on them
and nobody's watching to the battlefield

Theseus: where'd that come from

Medea: there
under your political thirsting crime

Theseus: don't assume meaning
happy with it
it's equated
it's on account

Chorus: early in his stride

Medea: what about the
blame

Chorus: and sincerely he replied

Theseus: manners

Aegeus: a single thought
wiped hardways

Theseus: like
American
white treemeaning

black mirrors laugh oil
retribution means
giving back praise

Chorus: again intensive music
killer weather
shuts the book

stopped in use
storied in use

Theseus: yet out of
solips
history

up jump selectivity
always go handways

a-applau-ause

a-applau-ause

faster – making it up   prove it prove it

did you get my drink

Medea: and the counterfuture
is closed in silent thinking

keeping them
coloc collab collat weapon

Theseus: should find a jumbled rabbit on the floor now
oh po-lise
rubbed appeared
indulging
my private movie

Medea: one peace
is violence
to carearms
my heavy

my young
who got
who was
readconstruct

this is why
arm of war
this song's
on the house

Theseus: he's in the library
he'll script us

Aegeus: where we patrimonious
an official prize

Theseus: judgment opposes
question and answer
tear him up
tear him down
on the world's platform
men disguised as dressed
disguise meaning wishes him up

siren up/down
sound

la-a-augh tra-a-
ack

sp-sp-sp-sp-sp

quickly

sotto voce to
Aegeus – they are
conspiratorial

Medea: by the time he keeps going over
             no edges show

Theseus: if it's not true how d'you know so much about it
Medea: it was told

Aegeus: what's today's date
Theseus: don't you see that in the paper

Aegeus: the light went on
             so should I

Theseus: you need to give a speech before I harvest down
             I'll unsavor in the classroom if they don't understand

Aegeus: as feathers stir time
             we've lived
             and each day round
             moves to its neighbors
             that we live at all
             is no murder
             there's no murder
             at all
             if we live at all

Medea: darts in my forehead

Theseus: I feared I gashed the world
             but it's a pained piety plaything

Aegeus: is that all there is to the dead?

             but where's the condition of change
             I just want to come so that I can plan my day

             ~~
Orpheus: **3 motives for Aegeus' rejuvenation**

Medea: warning
             half a day
             half a city
Chorus: and lays aside in drinking game

to M:

the ritual starts

SPEAKERS	TEXT	CHORUS
		in little mind
Aegeus:	no I'd do that	
Theseus:	sweet peas lace the office chair	
	I'm going fine I'm going fire	
Aegeus:	what'll you have	
	in your cowboy hat	
	tearing up the floor	
Theseus:	the words "that's so mine"	
Medea:	in the imagine all things yeast	
Aegeus:	there're always more words	
	life extinct of them	
Theseus:	deal	
Aegeus:	come howdare with you	
	trouble of the people	
Chorus:		night whirrs slow
		and clocks out
Medea:	we're turning to take it on	
	the full riddle conspires	
Chorus:		sitting to the right
		and to the wet of her
		toptable toomunch
		to bear
		hulligaloo lallay
Theseus:	trickles her	
Medea:	lap drinks	
Aegeus:	just one	
Chorus:		leans over
Medea:	it's closer than you think	
Chorus:		she leans over
Medea:	this was where to stop	
	and me in it	
	the black sea shits out of his	
Chorus:		so from his mouth
		scopes different
		grunted

225

(siren up sound)

The "choppers" lines
sound like helicop-
ters, a bass line.
"grows, falls" rises
and falls.
(to T):

grows, falls

grows, falls

grows, falls

grows, falls

(birds start
rhythmic
stomp)   grows, falls

grows, falls

grows, falls

grows, falls

grows, falls

away
Most birds stop.   grows, falls   sp-sp-sp-sp-
sp-sp-
grows, falls   sp-sp-
sp

Unison birds: away

SPEAKERS	TEXT	CHORUS
Medea:	voice	

~~

**Aegeus recognizes his own hilt as
Theseus draws his sword to carve**

Theseus:	penther	
	bullims	
	meat what I am	
	writing ceases on the open wall of heaven	
Chorus:		smites cooking-sword
		into wall of writing
Aegeus :	lumpsize firtrubing	
Theseus:	and what is the object?	
Medea:	it's a game	
	pap	
Aegeus:	so's tricked child	
Theseus:	I'm concluding	
	which holds a lot	
Chorus:	holds up the jug	
	to take a drink	
Aegeus:	the cups are cut like teeth	
Chorus:	he leans over	
Aegeus:	I resigned	
Chorus:	and puts it away	
Theseus:	why stop now	
Chorus:	speaks special spillage spare	
	spits speaking	
	spells pirates	
	in the mind	
Aegeus &	all I wanted was	
Theseus:	more	
Chorus:	so water flows away down the toilet	
Theseus:	darn	
	his lips and teeth say	
Aegeus:	young son boy lover	
	ages argue	
Medea:	his features fit like a fox	

the sound of
  choppers,
  the sound of
  choppers,
  the sound of
  choppers,
  the sound of
  choppers,
  the sound of
  choppers,
  the sound of
  choppers,
  the sound of
  choppers,
  the sound of
  choppers,
  the sound of
  choppers,
  the sound of
  choppers,
  the sound of
  choppers,
  the sound of

all on dayright treading

Aegeus: that's my redoubtable boy
               sameness stretched acabre
Theseus: what fahahathersize is this
               sizing him pastel
               past all
               doubtcaring
Aegeus: er er er
Theseus: rightness like cleaning
               er-minate dial kingsize

(to M):   and we'll meet you
               who slays at home hoping
               its first surface
               is silver again
               lick cheek

               ~~

Orpheus: **Medea takes the heat**

               this is the transformation
               what I've reaped
               and not only in my palm
               but shaking the whole hand
               like that
               I say
               excuse me for a moment
               and shut the door
               on my privacy

               like a folding intrick
               of a motherbird

               that's why I had to do something
               they have sin and they have high
               that's what I keep eating
               simple
               as if I had no
               city

               that's why they kept me here

this scene is said in
  unison, but with
  different meanings
  and intentions

T says "test
  ost
  erone"

it's not the wine of living
and it's not going home
it might be dear inventing
the difficult hillside

~~

Orpheus: **How Ariadne swung above the bull-dance, how**
      Theseus took her cord to get out of a tight maze, how
      he abandoned her on an island, and how he forgot
      not to kill his father

T to A, M to T: just a minute while I

leave the country for a few months

I'll let you know

I'll bring the
sown field

deft dext
her

drops me in

to my all body

it's a yarn

a trying
to tell

a test
ofst
her own

and I dropped her out

why so amazed

body all head
head all body

DIRECTIONS	BIRDS
(quite animal)	*(birds stomp rhythm)*

T to Ae:

T to A, then to M

T to M, M to T

T "bad"

T "mother"

SPEAKERS	TEXT	CHORUS

**(italics
T only):**   *snort* and I'll
travelravel

home

with my blood's

on the ground

in my blood

in the air

chuck yourself

reardrop

airpop

on the rocks

and leave my chair empty

old boy

and you'd better not
be here

for your slander
campaign

who's my bed

step

other

I've a good mind
to

badmouth

T bark, for M weave

your body

for everill

woof
because dog

warp
my way

a written
sheath

dress
for women

forever

knit from
enough rope

M to T: and excuse me

M to T, T to M: home
spun

M to T: un
fictioned

M to T, T to M: paid
out

M to T: I'll be back

in a millenium
or three

M to T, T to M: over your

dead
machine politic

interrupts:

SPEAKERS	TEXT	CHORUS
Chorus:		and turned
		liquid
A to M&T:	and excuse me excuse me	
T to A:	I need a running	
	jump	

~~~~

End of Part 5

The light on Athens overlaps into the first scene of the next part, during which Theseus takes his father's place and continues his speech-making silently with large aggressive gestures. The lit area in which he stands shrinks in size until it reveals only part of his face, then disappears.

Valda Setterfield

THE MEDEAD—ACT II
PART 6—MEDEA RETURNS TO THE EAST

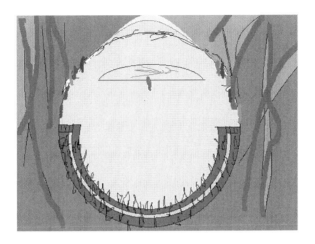

Medea Returns has a sense of horizontality (side to side), but recedes gradually to flat against the stage area by the time the film is playing. During the film, this Medea may echo the actress on film, or place herself in the landscape. At the last scene where she takes the "chair" (there is no literal chair), she turns to face the audience.

Orpheus: **The spiral winds the other way**

Medea: not without
loss

nor with
closing

nor backwards

comes done

a last passage

my own

for now

~~

Orpheus: **Medea in Crete**

Medea: whose silence is shed
whose shedding
backwards every
shed what forwards
she'd iter
uckray
spreading into our lithes
no wonder
longer it's threatened by
whonothing

o just get rid down
all I've lost
is totter
spell spelling
dearling I've undone

M's seashell dance

youshe they abandone
negligent eagerness fires done
while to abandon is all my
babe
lives be lives
take me away
there's no sluice left
I ought
to cray
jerluice
is a stammerer

why don't you just
ballocol

Chorus:

yes

it would be better if we crossed here

~~

Orpheus: **Medea in Africa**

Chorus:

drinks

water

pouring

into blue and clear

jars

seen from

the level of the table

bubbles of force

drop on the lens

her manymaking head

bend

back

who returned

at the end of her tether

to her mother

SPEAKERS	TEXT	CHORUS

being
and motherhaving

breathing through the ear

unsings shelly seashells
she tells
while creatures handopening

~~

Orpheus: **Medea in Troy**

Medea: where's my heart
not ignorance

a crashing cliff
its own rubble

misses the links
the sensible turns

when the straightest path
is an avoidance

the air is the song
and the blade swings
there

is the spasm to one
two

the knife is to blame
and the cure
and me

what repeats
is
the thread between

figuring
breath
through time

She breathes the film   aaaaahhhhh
projection on.   aaaaahhhhhh
                             aaaaahhhhh

to tissue
the differences
of the world

~~

Orpheus: **The catalogue of cloths**

Medea: one's the winning tapestry

one's the sheet
that tells in blood
the tongue raped of telling

one's the mazing
cloak of anger
stamped into place
one foot at a part of time
holding hands with another

one runs
logged with sweetness
a buzzing fleece
of golden future
appling down

one's the budded hair
of all our green ground

and one's these words
breath
misting night's everything
song overweaving her door
is her door
her endless skein
skinning her
till I see

what light catches
what shapes it

~~

DIRECTIONS	BIRDS
	(Birds are wind in this scene)
(M in the film is climbing a long rocky hill.)	whwhwhwhwhw
	whwhwhwhwhw
	hwhwhwhwhwh
	hwhwhwhwhwh
	whwhwhwhwhw
	whwhwhwhwhw
	hwhwhwhwhwh
	hwhwhwhwhwh
	whwhwhwhwhw
	whwhwhwhwhw
	hwhwhwhwhwh
	hwhwhwhwhwh
	whwhwhwhwhw
	whwhwhwhwhw
	hwhwhwhwhwh
	hwhwhwhwhwh
	whwhwhwhwhw
	whwhwhwhwhw
	hwhwhwhwhwh
	hwhwhwhwhwh
(Surveys from the top.)	whwhwhwhwhw
	whwhwhwhwhw
	hwhwhwhwhwh
	hwhwhwhwhwh
	whwhwhwhwhw
	whwhwhwhwhw
	hwhwhwhwhwh
	hwhwhwhwhwh
	whwhwhwhwhw
	whwhwhwhwhw
	hwhwhwhwhwh
	hwhwhwhwhwh
	whwhwhwhwhw
	whwhwhwhwhw
	hwhwhwhwhwh
	hwhwhwhwhwh
	whwhwhwhwhw
	whwhwhwhwhw
	hwhwhwhwhwh
	hwhwhwhwhwh

SPEAKERS	TEXT	CHORUS

Orpheus: **Medea in Persia**

Medea: I'm climbing the silver slope
to
hard but not indifferent

in premeditated violet

it's in the east and stunning

I feel a weight of workpelt

when there's no other there's place
speaking backwards
looking backwards
before place there's needful
and god hired
headmates

and everything forged
forced mesmiling
why I'm hillaway

here's the casual
manplate
here's my body
rubbing leaves

a step ahead
in my
assuming
.
I'm all over the place
so drop tears
place is what they're all over
over is what they're all

in spectacular place
city must lef

and stopped
in households

DIRECTIONS	BIRDS
	whwhwhwhwhw
	whwhwhwhwhw
	hwhwhwhwhwh
	hwhwhwhwhwh
	whwhwhwhwhw
	whwhwhwhwhw
	hwhwhwhwhwh
(M in film continues)	hwhwhwhwhwh
	whwhwhwhwhw
	whwhwhwhwhw

(M on film in a
  green place, many
  birds louder and
  louder on the
  soundtrack.)

                                        (birds echo
                                          vowels
                                          generally in
                                          this scene)

separate words, but
  said by several:

                              we
Just the birds for   we
  a bit.
                              we
                                                  we

                              oh we
                                                  we oh we

                              we
                                                  we

by the tight
thread
of my own
mother's
tie
to me

and the sooner I go
pech pech
the sooner I cup her

~~

Orpheus: **Medea in Colchis**

Medea: a rediscovery marigolds and flageolites
Chorus: we'll show you the title
                                                       right now listen

Medea: blue and gold
thicking power
flower

I saw in a book

I looked up
oh what a change

but in my closeyes

recognized her

and looked out
again

to a bird

who we

                    we who

do we?

                    we do

we we

                    oh oh

do we do we?

                    oh

oh we do oh we do

(birds crescendo,
    slightly   who who
    harsher)
we do we do we   me
    do we do we do   me
    do we?

(birds stop)

m-mm-mmm
    m mm mmm
    m-mm-mmm

The Mms lead to the
    title. She says it.
    From here on in
    Part 6 her scenes
    have no titles.
    (On film, Medea is   I!
    walking. We see
    the landscape and   me
    the abandoned   we!
    power and
    grandeur of the   we?
    former Soviet
    occupation.)

                    her

252

Chorus: she's coming she's
                                                                   poeet pfui
                                              and heart so weet weet weet abridged

Medea: perfection sprung
             all my holidays
             in a new image
             riot tongue
             let's string perfection
             it's too
             lize
             all pliant earth
             not this waking dayalize
             hard earth forestrungotten
             with birds' delays
             whose quieter
             playeaps

             whose strenuous tonguemurchery
             num mum
             mongue
             make me say my name
             flares up
             like silence in a crowd

             ~~
Medea: **M m m m em mmm**

             Medea in Aia

             a house in Motherwell
             brightness bursting
             the air
             while barrier stops
             birds don't
             o crue

             I look at her
             with her perfect trams
             oh grown fragile
             and the precious breath peching

her

*(The woman on
   film is walking by
   the sea.)*

her

being, a lone be

*(A train of oil tanks
   passes, loud)*

being, a bone be

254

friendship shore
changed her lifelive
lightning varying
mrs muck's makedo

kissed goodness out of her
like an orange in her hair

~~
takes her up
down among his obradobits
out to sea

sweet
ore thrown
casting by who she him
which wise upthrown
tick tape cant say
love other thrown

.

hugged heavy
post sweets to heaven
all my carclear
in her round body

.

and through her belief asked
when must I
what's next?
still on earth
I'm jecting
easel rubeyes

readily so she
nighttime has ead
all her ago
and bent summers
pretty dresses
filthy ribs
like legs sticking all up

all lorn away

(On film, now from M's p.o.v., a walk way, leaves overhead.)

hhhhhhhhhhhhh
hhhhhhhhhhhhh
hhhhhhhhhhhhh
hhhhhhhhhhhhh
hhhhhhhhhhhhh
hhhhhhhhhhhhh
hhhhhhhhhhhhh
hhhhhhhhhhhhh
hhhhhhhhhhhhh
hhhhhhhhhhhhh

d'you weep?
d'you?

(crosses a rough bridge and keeps walking) No *speaking for some moments.* Live *actress walks towards film.*

that's sayable

blows easily

but
where the material words
stop

another blood

is

love

but I'm breathless

olbalay
ons lovecredit marathon

let
go
your breath
and ache in things
and teach me
what sudden
smile
is this

lick spittle little
mothermouth
in dying dope
dip room for her
honeybreath
hitting heard
hearth heart
arthee her arthe heart

all hers

*(camera moves
across green and
up into the light)*

> *(birds fast
> stomping*

*(back in the rocky
place, M on film
enters a cavelike
area)*

*(M in film and M live
both sit facing
audience)*

*(The woman's voice
can be heard on
film below the live
voice. She is
speaking the same
text, in Georgian.)*

are her

coral
order

coming up for air

good
drum

~~
and she's still wielding
the two spoons
like drumsticks
come again

she say once
and for all there

knew
will know
chair

put yourself in it

Chorus: she
                                          shifts pronouns

how do things look

whether a son
whether a race
whether a battle

this
a woman's
tears for man

how he
says this
not that

that
telling

Film off.

Live M walks
  gradually to front
  of stage

                                                    papillon pupil
                                                      éparpillés

                                                    ha
crow laugh, one ha
  at a time

                                                    ha

                                                    ha

                                                    ha

                                                    ha

lets

can't see out of

but it's my skin

letting

be

~~
perform
last
sweet clock and identity

and sees nothing
but lids lips
sealed on
palpable

pauper paupiere purpurea
violet flies up in my face
camping ground in graveyard

the impossibly slow
laugh of the crow

bark worse than stick
in its throat

a winter of pictures
a night

such bravery
to stay
such bravery to go

softness taken

its place I can't
take its place away
that's next

stops walking

and all I lost
grayed
hurt
how teems
appear
no tread of nursing
deeper
than this it's
breach and breast and breath
and break

no further
that's further's all

~~~~~

End of Part 6

Nato Murvanidze, Valda Setterfield

THE MEDEAD—EPILOGUE

MEDEA IN HEAVEN

These few lines may be played by an additional (older) actress. All the cast are involved. Achilles can be played by Jason in a helmet or by the helmet alone. The women lined up behind Medea and the men behind Achilles.

The film comes back on. We see an empty theatre, with a door to the exterior at the back. Medea in the film comes through the door and walks slowly forwards over the stage and into a closeup.

The live Medea
  watches.

She turns back
  toward the
  audience, smiling
  and crying.

The other Medeas
  join her, as if one.

Achilles enters,
  crying too.

the marriage of tears

that's us that's me
I'm facing myself
with salt

tears of laughter
or tearing slaughter
into each others' eyes
all opposite

the unbearable children
I'm grave with
are your little picture
falling in every drop

I shed.

~~~

End of Play

The performers may leave through the audience,
or the audience though the stage.

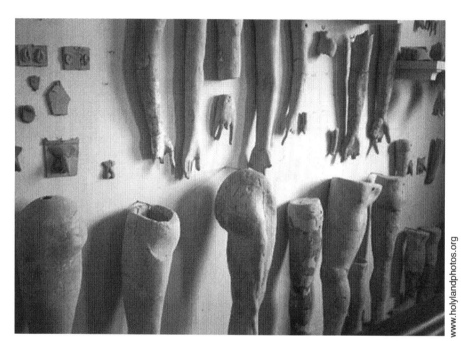

The Asclepion at Corinth

AFTERWORD

Do not all charms fly
At the mere touch of cold philosophy?
John Keats, *Lamia*[1]

I was drawn to spend time in the world of myth less for its narratives than for its multiplicity. In Pasolini's *Medea*[2], Jason meets a man who tells him "You can't see me any more"; we realise that this is the same figure who earlier in the film had the body of a horse, Cheiron, who raised Jason on the slopes of Mount Pelion. A centaur is now an image; I wanted to un-collapse those now familiar forms.

So anyone looking for my 'version' of the Medea story will find no single answer. The narrative here is the progression of a series of figures and stories, each appropriate to or expedient to its time, and ordered by the age of the respective figures of Medea. Why was such-and-such a story told at this point, or that? But each also bursts repeatedly, through the language, into its pasts and futures. Six women play Medea, and four men play eight men.

I was drawn to find the particular multiplicities of Medea on considering that the Medeas of the stage come mostly from the pens of men. She needed a female mouth and body, or several.

Writing this work, I made a journey of my own through all the cities of the epic, from the excavations at Vani in Colchis, to Iolkos, to Corinth, to Athens. And sea, and air. I also made other journeys, across some of my own passages of Medea, trials and exiles and births and deaths; back into our pasts; living the changing present of our own east-west relations; and through an immense vein of language.

By language I mean, first my own finding of the prosody of the work, inextricable from a method of generating it; intrinsic to that, a poetic breakdown of the imagery and morphologies of myth; and the etymological traces of its sounds.

The following essay is a summary of some aspects of the dramaturgy and poetics of *The Medead*. In scholarly terms, I will take some liberties, because the freedom of the poetic text is the driving force. The essay weaves together the following three lines of discourse:

- In the left-weighted column I orient the explanation to the moment in the performance epic that I'm referring to. I follow the order of the epic.
- In the central column I provide, for those less familiar with it, mytho-historical/ etymological/ theoretical background for my approach to the mythic material at that point. This is necessarily fuller at the beginning, for information.

- The right-weighted column describes some of the poetics and practical drama-
turgy of the performance work. Italicised passages are from directing notes to
the company, to indicate relationships between the larger structure of the piece
and its physical tropes for the performers.

I didn't write *The Medead* to illustrate these ideas. Nor does this essay explain the
play-cycle. These are the world in which it happens, among other ideas and worlds.
The Medead is an excavation out of spoken poetic material, and the Afterword an ex-
cavation out of what informed it. In writing this Afterword, deliberately after- and not
fore-, I know the slippages, elisions and gaps. I also know that these stories have been
told and told again. What I have to tell is in the language of *The Medead.* I took to
speech in the first place in the face of too much information. This is why the world of
the plays begins with nothing; and brings into being from there, and offers the made
thing.

~~

Prologue
(The cosmic world)

The world does not yet exist,
though perhaps only because we don't know it.

> The only existing fragment of the ancient Greek philosopher Anaximander,
> long before Socrates, is thought of as the first to describe a western cosmol-
> ogy. It may suggest[3] that he sees the beginning of the world, (which was not
> the first state of things), not only, as it had been interpreted, as order(liness)
> arising from chaos understood as undifferentiated matter, but as order (in
> time) arising from the cyclical, fixity arising from movement, things and
> seeing and naming arising out of ambiguity – a project of rationalising and
> separation that underpins our present culture.

> *Ambiguity. Being more than one thing. See Shattering.*

> This state of coming-into-being is a coming-into-appearance, appearance re-
> maining active.

The world does not yet exist,
though breath does.

> *Breathing: diastole and systole, as of light; as of the size of the 6*
> *parts of* The Medead, *back and forth between Medea alone or with*

others, particularly men; macro- and microcosm; how Part 1 is shaped, splits and grows, pulls back, splits and grows more, etc, till outwards.

Or birds do, or sounds.

We hear language in the calls of birds, as Aristophanes[4] did, as Farid ud-Din Attar[5] did, as Chaucer[6] did, because we both (we and the birds) have intention. In Homer, uttered and addressed speech is often winged, *epea pteroenta*[7]. In Ancient Egypt, a person's *ba-bird* was their soul[8]. We mimic birdsong and the birds mimic us. We hear music in the songs of birds because we both know the ecstasy of a continuous present.

Chapman tells us of Homer[9] as a child whose "nurse... from whose breast oftentimes, honey flowed in the mouth of the infant – after which, in the night, he uttered nine severall notes or voices of fowles, viz. of a Swallow, a Peacocke, a Dove, a Crow, a Partrich, a Red-Shank, a Stare, a Blackbird, and a Nightingale."

Samita Sinha, conceiving of the music for *The Medead*, made a 6-part contemporary raga cycle, partly following the cycle of the day. Using primarily vocals, a drone machine, and a tanpura, she moved through time.

The world does not yet exist,
though she does.
She speaks and the world comes into existence.
Language, like light, makes the invisible become
visible, covers its invisible contours, gives it form,
its own form.

Invisible: dark; possible/latent; not perceptible but occupying space or time, so either with a before and an after or taking up an area not able to be occupied by anything else; the scenically ob-scene; inside, internal; either made visible by the performers by being looked at, or invisible by not being looked at; or visibly invisible by looking away.

In Greek myth, Medea was of the family of the sun. But light has many moments. Her father Aeetes was the eagle, soaring against the light. Medea's moment was the first steps of the day, born through darkness from the east she faced, guarding its portal.

271

So she waited in the night; no not waited but spoke, spoke and listened in the dark till those words made appear.

But Medea was not a Greek.

We are not in Greece.

> *The actors are first, people, then performers as they become distinguished from the audience, and lastly, characters, through what they say and do; these are fluid, changeable.*

M, Me, Ma, the mouth opens. From the center out, comes life. Ma, Maia, Sanskrit for mother, Mary, May, Maryam, Mahi (whose other name is Bharati, goddess of speech)[10] The mother opens. *Metra*[11] in Greek[12] is the womb or the entrance to the womb, and *meter* is mother. *Metro*n is measure. This is not only the measure of a ruler, off into the distance, but patterning and growing measure, as we feel in the ceilings of the Alhambra, or in plants. It is the returning measure of poetry or dance. (And all that said, in Georgian Mama means father; the word for mother is deda. Etymology gets slippery.) But there is also another set of meanings: Metis was an ancient figure of Wisdom, later the name for a goddess of wisdom whom Zeus swallowed. *Medon* is one who rules, or guardian, as is medousa. *Medomai* is to plan, think about, be mindful, and *medos*, only used in plural *medea*, is counsels, wiles, or care as in caring for. Medea the figure is spelled *Medeia*, seen later as queen of Media in ancient Persia. A Mede (one from Media) is Medikos. But then there is no one thing to find. Medicine as a drug was actually farmakon, also the name for the sacrificial scapegoat. Or ram. A cure can be iasis, as in perhaps Jason.

Following back into other cultures, the double meaning of the word Medea, "the root of which, mad, is in the names of Medusa and of Andromeda... mean[ing] both the genitals and thought. Its root is mad = to dissolve. It forms the latin madeo = to be wet, sanscrit madati = to be drunk, Zend mada = inspiration due to drunkenness, and very probably the English mad."[13] This line of thought leads too in Greek to meth-, contrasted in methodos and in methe, wine (or mead, from honey, Madhu in the Rig Veda). Heady stuff indeed. Medea has aspects of both Andromeda and later Medusa, but for now is before both of them.

She neither sees nor is seen.

Samita Sinha's music for *The Medead*, fusing her knowledge of classical Indian vocals and contemporary experimental sound, stretches the sonic landscape of the work to a scope reflecting its language(s).

The female Georgian musicologists who formed the ensemble *Mzetamze*[14], dedicated exclusively to the musical traditions of Georgian women, write: "Mzetamze means "sun of suns", a mythological name indicating female origins: 'The sun laid down and bore the moon', says [one of their recordings]." They make the distinction that the songs in Georgian society sung exclusively by men have "representative functions" whereas women's songs are tied to ritual and the life cycle. They write of the "Cradle-songs" or Nana: "cradle songs are not only for putting children to sleep; the moment of falling asleep is purported to be fraught with danger... thus cradle songs contain elements of ritual: *ghughuni* (cooing) or *ghighini* (quiet singing to oneself in an especially low vocal range)... Often the word nana constitutes the entire text", or other lines "without determinable meaning". Nana, they say,[15] is the Great Mother; nana means mother in the Megrelian and Lazian dialects of Georgian.

In Celtic Scotland, the power of women's poetry was so feared that Màiri McLeod was banished from Skye – a child's life could not stand the weight of her panegyric.[16] The very quality of their speaking was active, might harm. Forbidden to sing to the children they nursed, they instead termed their songs *cronan* or croon, pretended that what they sang had no meaning, was only nonsense words, parts of words. They would not name things, acquisitive. But these words have body, have movement, are experienced, are time. Ho ree ho ro. Nani nana. Lulla lulla.

And let's return to where we were: a world being born.

"The Greek for 'to bring forth or to produce' is tikto... The Greeks conceive of *techne*, producing, in terms of letting appear."[17] And to engender or give birth. From *tikto* come our words textile and text. Making involves a patterning, a rhythm or *kosmos*. The *kosmos* is what covers, such as the armour of men or the adornment of women. The *chros* in Homer is the skin or colour, not as in the dermis as of a flayed animal, but "the living body understood as a surface and the bearer of visibility... Appearing was an active surface, with *epiphaneia* a word used for both... As *kosmos* clothes the body to make it appear, kosmos clothes the ground [in a dance] in order to make it appear." So in appearing there is time and movement. "The divinity of the Greek gods rested on their always appearing... this...is what resided in the scintillating surface of the *daidalon*" (the thing that is made, as in Daedalus, the artist). The woven *daidala* were *poikilon*, the texture catching the light, changing. "Once a year the *xoanon* [the wooden image] of the Samian Hera was unbound and hidden in a willow tree, where it was then rediscovered and brought back to its shrine... This ancient ritual would also have been a yearly revelation of appearing and reappearing as the essence of all that is divine,

athanatos" (deathless).
If Medea is a woman in a story, first she is a girl, here on the verge of the passage,
though if Medea is a woman in myth, first she is an older woman, in the
sense of an older version of that woman.

A child who speaks as a child yet knows something of what words might do.
In Greek an epode is a spell, a song over, ep- (over) and ode (song, poem).
(And the word of the oracle is epos, a faculty ascribed to Medea in Pindar[18];
her words are "breathed" from "an immortal mouth").

Medea "sings a skin of language over the invisible."

She feels the power of her language to set fire to the night. And does. So her father
arrives, speaking in a different language, the language of the symbol literalised. When
the birds flurry up at his approach, it is "the *word* birds" that flies around. Aeetes is
an eagle. The gold in the tree is a ram.

Part 1/1
Medea in Aia
(the mythic world)

Birds not only speak, they know, too. Who can see better, flying above, looking far
off? A coming storm, a running prey. Their element is air, which is also song.

> Perhaps we can visualise Aeetes like the Bird-headed divinity of Assyrian
> reliefs[19]; his animal neighbours might have been the winged lions of Ancient
> Mesopotamia, or of Achaemenid reliefs[20], the lioness demon of Proto-
> Elamite Iran[21]. But at the northeast edges of these ancient empires lay the
> steppes, the lands of shamanism. Shamans worldwide wear feathers and
> skins, their animal selves. The wearing of animal hides might enhance the
> contents of dreams[22]. Heracles in his lionskin, the man in the panther skin,
> even Jason according to Pindar[23] when he first came from his upbringing by
> a centaur, are heroes yet wear another self. The flying of the shaman[24] is not
> only an ecstatic experience, but also an encounter with death. The bird is
> both harbinger and psychopomp, and in taking on its qualities the shaman
> can cross to the other world to intervene on behalf of a community.

This Medea wants these powers, though maybe she has them already, fledgling,
untested.

Then alone again. Female rites of adolescent passage can be savage, often to do with restriction. She wants to shed. She must change in order to be.

> *Passage: movement to next stage of life: or to next generation;*
> *historical change; (at least) one in each of the 6 Parts. See Rejuve-*
> *nation. The boundary is another level of being.*

And into this world, having sailed into the gateway of the river that is European and Asian, comes the Greek, Jason.

And he brings place. The *Argonautika*[25], or Voyage of the Argo, tells of his quest for the Golden Fleece, to bring it to Greece, and with it, his unplanned prize, Medea, the figure of the foreigner, from the east like light from the dark. The writer of the extant Argonautika, Apollonius of Rhodes, was late in the history of Greece, compared to Homer. The story, however, is older than Homer, who refers to it as well known[26]. The epic describes the journey of Jason and the ship into her country, the land of Colchis, up the marshy delta of a great river, the Phasis. On a possiblemap of Anaximander[27], the Phasis would be one of the three bodies of water on the earth (besides the surrounding Okeanos) separating the three land masses: the Mediterranean separating Europe from Libya, the Nile separating Libya from Asia, and the Phasis separating Europe from Asia; at the center of the map would be Hellas (Greece), and at its centre Delphi, the navel of the earth.

Colchis is to this day the name for Western Georgia, where the triangle created by the Upper and Lower Caucasus Mountains meets the Black Sea. The great Georgian epic, *The Man in the Panther's Skin*[28], tells of an opposite journey, to rescue a beloved woman, Neshat-Daredjan, who has been stolen to the west. She is described as like the sun, like the moon. (If Jason's voyage resembles Odysseus' in its departure and return to Greece, Medea's, like Neshat-Daredjan's, is its opposite; Homer was countering Medea's epic.) The Georgian poet tells us that his epic is a Persian tale. The Persia of his time (12th c) was Muslim since a century, of course much later than the Persian Empire that was the enemy of Greece in the last half-millennium BC, itself later than the ancient civilisations of the region, Persis, Sumeria, Assyria, Mesopotamia (that greater marshy river plain, now drained by Saddam Hussein), its cities of Babylon and Ur. Maybe then we can come to a past of the figure of Medea.

But time was flexible for those Greeks, or was it that the figures themselves were not single? Or did these civilisations, not just in the near East but from the Mediterranean to the Indus, unlike the later Greeks, in early times embrace more the cycle than history[29]? Herodotus begins his *Histories*[30] by answering

275

his own question of the origin of the Greek-Persian conflict by enumerating a series of woman-stealing episodes in each direction: Io to the east, Europa to the west (both of whom the Greek myths saw as cows), Medea to the west and finally Helen to the east. Seriously? For a decade of war with Troy, and centuries with the Persians? Besides the fact that Herodotus comments that the women must have been asking for it so it didn't count as rape? So for now let's close this journey back and east as duly having undermined the historical value of the Greek and Roman versions of the stories, but more valuably perhaps having undermined the usefulness of history or geography or person at all in the matter of Medea. What we do have is language, though differently.

When I travelled to Georgia to see how the world looked when its centre shifted, Europe and India now equidistant, I was told that the word for a Greek is Berdzeni, barbarian, and the word for a Georgian is Kartveli, happy. And found that far from being the evil witch and murderess of Greek fame, Medea is the patron of medicine, whose image appears on the windows of homeopathic pharmacies.

And from being alone, she is now being watched.

> *Stranger(s): depends who you are; here, in particular east for west and west for east; here, invoke paradigm shifts.*

Coming up the delta, Jason saw evidence of the strangeness of the people, including graves above ground with the dead standing up; coming up the delta towards Samtredia, I saw cemeteries and houses with life-sized paintings and cut-out photographs of the dead standing up.

The civilisation of Aeetes' city Aia, if such ever existed as the Greeks describe it (the word Colchis was later), was destroyed by invasion and war[31] with its neighbours. In Georgia, some say it is the rich archeological site at Vani, which its archaeologist Otar Lordkipanidze conjectures may have been a temple of Dionysos. Some say it is present-day Kutaisi; the Argonautika refers to Medea's father as "Kytaian Aeetes".

The river was the Phasis in Ancient Greek; phasso is to cleave; but phasis is speech, a sentence. Jason himself, Jeson in the *Argonautika*, is a man of few words, of action. A bit of a show-off, in Pindar[32].

We don't know that yet. At least in western narrative form, we don't; in cyclical narrative form, we do know what has not yet happened.

But he brings with him Orpheus.

> This is not simply the sweet singer of later myth, but from an older tradition. *Orphanos* is one bereft, as in our orphan; and *orphnaios* is dark, dusky. Orpheus is an unusual figure in Greek myth in that he has no place in the genealogies, but is more likely an import from another culture[33], with 4 separate stories of Orpheus in classical times: "(i) Birds and animals came to hear him perform...(ii) He took part in the Argonautic expedition and saved the Argonauts from the seduction of the sirens by outsinging them. (iii) He prevailed upon the infernal powers to release his wife from Hades. (iv) He was assassinated by a party of Thracian women...They cut off his head but it continued to sing...The stories portray him not as a distant forerunner of Homer, but as a singer of a different type: one who can exercise power over the natural world, and who can countermand death itself, a 'shamanistic' figure." Further, the name is associated with a Dionysiac cult with elements of shamanism (descent to hell, ritual dismemberment, ecstasy, female hieratics) standing in some opposition to the Apollonian, and his later form may be a kind of domestication to Apollo. The through line is song.

> Going back, Orpheus begins to disappear as a figure and to become the Orphic, an adjective applied to texts of a particular theogony, tracing the origins of the world and its gods, though these are to some extent the same thing. In one version of this, unaging Time is first, generating Aither, Ananke, Chasm and Night, followed by Phanes (meaning as we know 'appearing') springing radiant from an egg, and who is of both sexes, self-generating another Night, and from their union come the Titans earth (Ge), sky (Uranos), sun and moon; further theogony follows, via Kronos (Time as ordered) through to Zeus, who swallows Phanes and is thus the only king. In this and other versions Phanes has other names, including Protogonos and Metis, later identified as female. In another version Night herself is first. This is the pre-Zeus cast of characters, different to the classical Hesiodic theogony[34], more fluid in nature, in relation, more identified with primal matter; and more like the near Eastern genealogies. Not that Zeus was a new Greek invention; he is Dyaus in the Rig Veda[35]. Though later Greek Orpheus was Thracian, the Orphics may have had a Minoan origin[36], which would mean an Egyptian or Eastern Mediterranean past.

Jason and Orpheus' interest in Medea, then, and hers in each of them, is very different.

> If appearing is essentially a becoming, active, then Zeus seems the god of greater fixity; even if he has the power to change (generally for disguise the purposes of rape). But this is the Zeus we inherit from Ovid, a Roman; earlier

Greek Zeus had multiple forms and names. The ancient Greek world stretches over a long period, and its archaic cultures are sometimes only guessed at by its classical tellers. Ovid, even later, opens the final book of The Metamorphoses with a Pythagorean speech[37] on the mutability of forms. Much Orphic material was adopted into Pythagoreanism. (Pythagoras was from Samos, a Thracian island). The egg made by Unaging Time, from which Phanes springs is a non-Greek element, linked to Phoenician, Zoroastrian and Indian cosmogonies, and the Egyptian eternal sun-god Re[38]. In Homer, the first parents are not Uranos and Ge but Okeanos and Tethys, more resembling the Babylonian couple Apsu and Tiamat, not Indo-European but of Semitic Mesopotamia, the sweet and the salt waters[39]. Uranos was drugged and castrated by his children, and Apsu was put to sleep by "the word that charmed the waters"[40], bound and killed by the children who were inside himself and Tiamat. We'll get back to Apsu and dismemberment later.

When Orpheus sings in the earlier books of the Argonautika, he is describing genealogies, a way of giving identity. It is just where Medea was supposedly from that friction between Near Eastern and Indo-European genealogies might occur.

To Orpheus from Thrace in northeastern Greece were also attributed spells and other shamanistic material. Plato speaks in *The Republic* of Orpheus' "hubbub of books"[41], and is not that detached head, still speaking after death, the very image of a book? This is the logos, not the lyric.

Orpheus brings much to Medea in his severed songs.

His knowing is the knowing of interpretation. Three kinds of knowing can be identified in ancient Greek: *gnonai* is to know the significance of something; *eidenai* is to have seen; *epistethai* is to have skill.[42]

First she hears, and then she sees. But she does not know what she is listening to or that it is outside of herself; and she does not know what she sees or whether it is what she feels.

Here come language and the body. So *The Medead* has to be a performed work.

Until Orpheus appears, the titles of the scenes are spoken shared across the performers, they are not enunciations by subjects[43]. After he appears, even after he dies, he speaks these titles. These titles are where the story lies; some, especially when Orpheus sings, are like trailers, or 18th-19th-century chapter summaries (*in which our hero…etc.*).

Orpheus, collector of origins, wants hers, and offers her origins in return, each a knife,

a catalogue of them, as Homer's catalogue of ships in the Iliad[44], and as his description of Achilles' shield in the Iliad[45] so like Anaximander's map of the world[46], and which we fly over and zoom into as if in a special effects film. These knives are birds, and songs too, all inhabitants of the air. The Greek for sword was aor, which hangs in the air. They are her dowry.

> *Knives: on one hand, song, what goes through the air; what creates the split, the shattering; also change, Kali's violence; power.*

What Jason wants is The Golden Fleece. What is that?

The Greek mythical narrative will be told in more detail in Part 3, *Medea in Iolcos*, when Medea arrives with Jason in his homeland. By then, in any case, the story will have fixed more into a pageant of images.

For now, the fleece hangs in a tree and is what Medea saw as the first light caught it, reflective, dazzling, appearing itself, brought to light by the covering of her words.

For Jason the Greek, the ram whose skin he seeks arrived with Phrixos. His ancestor Athamas, to save his crops, was ordered to sacrifice his children by Athena, but his wife Ino placed them on the back of a ram that leapt across the sky to land in the east. Helle (light), after whom the Hellespont was named, fell to her death, but her brother Phrixos survived and having landed in Colchis, sacrificed the ram in thanks. He gifted its golden skin to the king, Aeetes of Colchis, and settled in marriage with the king's daughter Chalkiope, Medea's older sister. The skin therefore belongs to Jason's family and he must bring it back. This is the telling of a later, heroic age, the hero having to execute a cosmic task[47] (bringing back the sun).

But what is it?

The Golden fleece in the Argonautika is *chryseos koas*; koas is fleece, khovas or tkhov in Georgian[48]. The fleece is also referred to as *auton*, which can also mean the finest linen, recalling the covering that makes appear. *Chryseos* or *chryseios* is golden, *chryseion* is anything made of gold, also precious money or treasure, including metaphorically. *Chrio* is to anoint, or to colour. Why is this dazzling light a ram's skin?

In Persian legend, the hvarnah or kvarrah is translatable[49] as "the imperial glory of Iran", and features throughout Persia's long history. The Khvarenah[50] is the "Awful Royal Glory", it is a thing (because there is an attempt to steal it), the possession of which conveys sovereignty, and first appears in the dream of Cyrus[51]. In the Shahnameh[52], the epic of the Kings of Persia, the blacksmith Kavah complains against the tyrant Zahhak or Zohak, and raises an army, by tying his leather apron, made from the skin of a ram, to a spear. This is greeted by the hero Faridun as the flag of Kavah, a royal standard, and he eventually conquers the tyrant.

The ram in the Zodiac is Aries,[53] the first sign. To trace its cross-cultural meanings: as a hieroglyph it is the male organ, the engendering principle. It corresponds in Vedic doctrine to Agni, meaning fire, heat as life-force and as the first sacrificial fire. The Ram in Sanskrit is Uranah or Urnos. In Gothic it is Widdr, as in German wieder or again. It has the same root as Agnus, the lamb, as in Christian Easter and Judaic Passover rites, and is the agent of the cycle of death and rebirth. The Egyptian sun-god Amon-Ra, (or Re) has the head of a ram (in the 1st and 2nd millennia BC into AD); he was creator of all the other gods, not unlike Uranos who in Greek myth was seen as the father of the gods. Sanskrit Vrsan is male, engendering. Ur indicates origin, and in Hebrew Aur is light; in Latin uro is to burn.

The Caucasus mountains, bordering Colchis to the north and south, are where Prometheus was chained to live out his endless punishment, the one who stole fire to give to mortals. The Argonauts, approaching Aia by sea, hear his cries from the mountains[54]. Prometheus may also be *Pramanthu*[55] of the *Bhagavad Purana*; the pramantha in the *Rig Veda* is the stick used to ignite the sacred fire, Agni. In the *Rig Veda*, Indra is the ram, but they are also addressed as a dual deity[56]. Some stories of Prometheus are also told of Hephaestos, the artist of the Greek gods, the smith, the Tvastar of the Rig Veda[57] and of the family of the similar, more Cretan, Daedalus.

Sergei Paradjanov, the Georgian film director, shows the Prometheus figure as Amirani, a folk-hero[58][59]. In Georgia I needed only to go around the back of the mountain church to be offered a drink to a flame and a strangled chicken; this is Jado, older than the church.

As I wrote *The Medead*, the ram for me was the small but breathtaking golden ram found at Ur, from the 3rd millennium BC, and though sometimes called a goat, it is also titled "the ram in the thicket" as in the story of Abraham; raised on its hindlegs, its pelt and horns of lapis-lazuli, peering through a gold flowering tree[60].

Medea is not the Golden Fleece. But between what Orpheus wants and what Jason wants, perhaps she is.

> *Skin: the covering/veil of materiality; the power of language and the creative, like the conjuror's hankie; how light makes visible, light as a clothing; the act of appearing, cf Arrival; animal; the vulnerability of, and the sign of, the scapegoat; later, visible ethnicity;*

The principal sacrifices of the Rig Veda are the producing of fire from friction, and the pressing of the sacred Soma juice (pre-Dionysiac[61]), which is then filtered through threads of wool or fleece, sometimes "shouting" in the process, sometimes mixed with mead[62]. But at the end of the book are two Hymns on Creation, referring to an older, mysterious primeval sacrifice, before the gods: in the world as one and therefore nothing rises the first impulse, desire, and the world is divided in two by a thread; then there is a weaving; hymns were the shuttles, and the first creation was Speech or Voice, which could communicate between heaven and earth[63].

Veda, knowledge, is a cognate of Medea and Metis, with the m-v shift of many branches of Indo-European, including Gaelic.

As the time of the symbol, the animal, intervened into Medea's elemental time with the arrival of Aeetes, now the time of the hero intervenes. She runs back.

Part 1/2

And into the house of Aia, "on the pictured couch"[64], the plenty of an animate table, where fruit is flesh and nuts have brains, come the strangers.

It is Ideia's table, her mother, or Eidyia[65]

> as in the word *eidenai* to see and to know (above), from which our "idea". She is not active in the Argonautika, or even mentioned in Euripides; for *Apollonius*, however, she is part of establishing *Medea's* divine genealogy. The opposite to her name is Hades, ruler of the underworld, hell itself, or not-seeable[66].

It is Orpheus who speaks for the newcomers, offers another song, the unsuitable but prophetic tale of Philomela[67], with its neglectful husband, its infanticide, its vengeful women; and violence to a woman's voice.

> In Sandys' Ovid: "...my voice shall breake / through these thick walls and

teache the woods to speake"[68], are Philomela's last words before Tereus cuts out her tongue.

But this Medea licks her lips at song.

> *Trailer-title: some scene-titles are mini-narratives, like a play-within-a-play. Though they preface their supposed telling, this is usually a song and refers rather than tells, so the titles bear the burden of telling. Usually a foreshadowing.*

This song provokes the official encounter between Jason and Aeetes, and Aeetes' challenge. On another level the meeting is one of desire. Medea wants to run away with the band.

> *Freeze: a stopping of time; a rendering of the invisible; scenically, often (at a shattering) with a very directed gaze, either eyes only, to focus on someone/thing, or whole head turn; can give the clarity for a shattering-shift; see Looking away.*

Her seeing of Jason barely sees him, sight seeing itself,

> like Titania seeing Bottom, who didn't really need a second ass's head[69]. Isn't it actually Titania who had the dream? If she is, as Zukovsky says,[70] Bottom's dream, then it is a dream of her dreaming. He is a weaver.

> Jason, in the text and directing of *The Medead*, can look at but not return the gaze of Medea. He sees her as what he doesn't have.

> *Looking away: not seeing, or something is unseeable; looking out to the diastole.*

In Pindar's telling, it is not Eros but the "dappled wryneck"[71] that Aphrodite sends to spark the relation between Medea and Jason, who "then burned in her heart". The wryneck or iynx is a bird which can turn its head completely; it is tied across a wheel and played as an instrument, an image of torture, and creates madness. It is also Ixion, tied to the wheel, an image of the sun bound daily in its burning course across the sky[72].

In the Argonautika, Jason's hero-task is that he must yoke the fire-breathing bulls to plough the field of war, and sow the dragon's teeth from which will spring armed men whom he has to cut down.

But here Aeetes says that more economically.

In the early 20th century much myth was interpreted as symbolic of and embodying rituals invoking the success of agrarian processes; Jason's task would have been ploughing, sowing and reaping a harvest in one day.[73] Jason's "winning of the golden fleece is paralleled by Heracles' winning of the golden apples, which another unsleeping dragon guarded." A hero is the hero.

The conflation of apples and a fleece in a tree is not so distant in ancient Greek: Melon[74] is a fruit, an apple first, melos medikos a citrus fruit, and others. A sheep is also melon, or a goat. Melos is a song, whence melody. Melissa is the bee, a word also applied to poets, and to the oracular priestesses of Delphi. Melos is a limb too. But melas is black, dark. What colour were these apples, this fleece? We all know a story of a tree in which there hung a fruit, guarded by a snake. And on limbs, more later.

The shamanistic tree[75] joins the lower to the upper world, like Jacob's ladder, or Yayoi Kusama's . In the upper rooms in the palace of Knossos[76] in Crete, a central pillar fanned out as the heavens[77].

The word metis is used for both Jason and Medea's wisdom. She knows how to do things; he knows how to get other people to do them. (Which is why Zeus swallowed Metis. Besides, it is fairly accepted that mythic narratives of battles or conquering often personify the introduction of a new religious or cultural focus, supplanting an older god or gods. So do all Zeus' rapes enact f*ing the female deities? Medea refused him – but look what happened to her reputation). Anyway, Jason could not have completed his brute task without Medea's strategic instructions and her knowledge of plant medicines, against her family's interests. And yet in the Argonautika she is depicted from one scene of tears to another (and in her dream she thinks that she, not the fleece, is the golden prize[78]).

Her potion to protect Jason is distilled from the plant, resembling a crocus, that sprang in the Caucasus from the blood of Prometheus[79], and preventing wounds from having effect. At the cave city of Uplistsikhe in Georgia, the ancient oracular centre where we filmed for Part 6 of *The Medead*, we are shown the stone medicine store where traces of herbs were found. Today in western medicine colchicine is a derivative of the Colchian crocus.[80] Krokos is the crocus; but Krokys is the pile, or nap, of cloth or wool.

In one of Uccello's paintings of George and the dragon (Ge-org, the one who works the earth, the farmer), the maiden, unruffled in her flowing dress, seems to be holding the dragon by a leash while George, mounted and armoured, pokes it in the eye at lance's length at the mouth of its cave; with a dejected eye it dribbles blood onto a few squarish patches of greenery. In a later one the fields look more civilised, George and his horse are bigger than the dragon that dances towards his lance in its throat, the anemic maiden is not tethered to the dragon or vice versa and the cave has shrunk to the appearance of a small tent. The dragon is the chthonic animal, but then so is the woman. It is also the sensual, sexual. Medea's is more likely to be a snake[81].

So when "Medea lulls the fleece-guarding dragon for Jason", in the language of *The Medead*, which is after all where it all happens, there is no difference between his taking of the animal and of her. But it is she who tames.

The rest, to the sea, is blurred action movie. And a distance beyond which the eagle can not fly.

> *Tears: a shattering; a mirror, a good wash, a tide; for a woman, heat like blood.*

The title of the final scene of Part 1 of *The Medead*, *The sea surrounds and disperses like the limbs of her brother Apsyrtus pursuing*, collapses an important mythic reference. In the pre-performance version there was a scene now omitted for dramatic reasons, entitled *Medea severs sibling ties*, in which her brother Apsyrtus (and sister Chalkiope) also appear. Apsyrtus in the *Argonautika* pursues her and Jason fleeing in the ship Argo. Jason persuades Medea to call him aboard and kills him. In ritual atonement Jason dismembers him, spattering blood on Medea's dress, and they bury him, giving his name to the place. We are told by Apollodorus[82] that the murder happened when the brother was a child, taken by Medea as they left. The parts of his body were thrown overboard so that Aeetes would be slowed in his pursuit by having to bury each at a time. The notes to the Penguin version of the Argonautika comment that there is no known etymology for the name Apsyrtus. Greek etymology, that must be. Early tribes in the region had the names Aphaz, Apsil, Apšil, Apsua, Abazaha, Abaza[83]. I hear in it also Apsu, the water god of the Bablyonians, his myriad children inside him, who contained and killed him.

In the *Argonautika*, Apsyrtus receives from the Greeks the new name of Phaethon [84], *shining*. Phaethon son of Eos, the early eastern sun, was a sun-hero; but Phaethon son of Helios, the bright sun, was killed by a bolt from his father as he rose, fell and, like Apsu, drowned in the marshes[85].

The sound combination SPR is identified with the ram[86]; "it is found among others in Greek words: spargan, to be swollen with sap, or desire;... spairo, to palpitate;... sparasso, to tear apart;... in English: sprout, spray, spring." We can add sperm, spurt, and note further the sense of distribution in the movement of all these words, an energy that bursts out, grows, scatters or multiplies. *Spao* is to draw, pull, convulse, swell, be pregnant, drink in, enjoy. The ritual dismemberment and arrangement of the parts of an animal was sparagmos; also linked to the ancient analysis of poetry; the text of a poem as the body in sacrifice, the song an exchange replacing the body[87]. In Latin apsus, from which our apse, is a vault or curve, as Apsu is the surrounding original waters of the earth, like Okeanos. Like the Vedic Aptya, the Watery[88], who lived at the outer limit of the world. In the Akkadian creation myth[89] Apsu is the vastest, the deepest, an abyss. "Apsu is the semitic form of Sumerian Abzu, both the ocean, the abyss and the uttermost limit"[90] , but though we may be told that "any similarity between Greek abussos abyss, unfathomable, and Abzu or Apsu is pure coincidence", the *Medead* considers an alternative culture to the Greek in a story of a foreigner. It is what they did not know. And it's in my ear. The first words of the Akkadian creation myth are "When there was no earth, no heaven, no height, no depth, no name, when Apsu was alone.."[91] The particular child who overpowers him is Ea, god of the earth and of wisdom, who wears a "flaming glory coat"; and "the *usrat* created by Ea to overcome Apsu is both a powerful spell and an intellectual design; it is an adumbration of the form of the universe which does not yet exist but which may exist... It is a difficult word to translate, but "artifice" may suggest the fragility of something that still belongs to the world of thought"[92]. We might see it through the lens of the notion that making as a form of knowledge, episteme, preceded but was not less valuable than eidenai, having seen, or sophia, which by Plato had lost its body[93]. It was episteme that allowed epiphaneia.

Even after Apsu is killed he still exists, holy[94]. He is drowned, though he is water. Apsos is also a limb.

When Jason throws his parts into the sea he returns Apsyrtus to himself.

Part 2
Medea on the Argo
(the heroic world/the colonising world)

Isaac Newton noticed that the Voyage of the Argo draws a Zodiac[95], through its encounters with the Ram Phrixos, the Bulls of Aeetes, the Dioscuri twins, etc.

For Medea here the cycle is not visible. This is a unilinear voyage, it is narrative. Can we move faster now, blown across the Black Sea?

> It was actually not our Black Sea that the Greeks renamed the Hellespont, sea of light, supposedly after Helle; in *The Iliad* the Hellespont may be limited to the Dardanelles straits, preceding even the Sea of Marmara[96]. In the Odyssey, whose ports of call may anyway be fictional, The Black Sea is simply Pontos, the sea. The name of the Black Sea may be traced[97] to akshaena, dark coloured, in the language of ancient Iran, mostly land-locked. The Greeks domesticated this by their similar-sounding *axenos* or inhospitable, uninhabitable; and changed it again, for the sake of an oracle[98], to Euxenos, hospitable (or to placate their growing trade partners along its southern shore). It is in modern times that we have returned to the Persian. I wonder how it appeared from its northern shores, the shamanic lands.

> Apsu was sweet water, of the marshy deltas, Tiamat salt. Apsu was contained, his powers killed by his children: silt, the horizons, the heavens and Ea, wisdom. We leave him behind, in the limen, marsh or harbor, though he follows part way, in a storm from the east.

> But perhaps the historical expedition of Jason, some time in the 13th century BC, never left the Mediterranean[99]. The Argonautika could be a conflation of a tradition from Iolcos (Part 3 of *The Medead*), with a famous pirate raid on Troy, and a Minyan tradition of Phrixos son of Minyas. In this interpretation Medea was then not even eastern.

>> But tellings attract tellings, similar women become one, one multiplies, and speech makes its own world.

> Also, poets sometimes give listeners what they want to hear (particularly in the days when they were paid). Pindar and Euripides, major makers of the classical Greek episodes of the story of Medea, wrote for competitions and patrons. The list of Argonauts is chronologically impossible too. And the mapping of their ports of call, Zodiacal as it may be, is also colonising – we were here, and we built here, and we named here.

> None of this, however, means that there was no influence from the east, the mass of which stretches thousands of miles from the first eastern port of Troy. While in Georgia some of the Medea tradition may be a back-formation from the Greek, some is clearly, as the stolen Naredjan-Neshat of the *Man in the Panther Skin*, Persian; or as shown above, less personified still. Georgia is a very late name, and Colchis late too though less so. The local tribes

came under Mongol and Sumerian sway. The Argo may relate to the Ark. Ancient Sumeria too had a deluge myth, its survivors in a huge boat[100]; and the Babylonian version of the Gilgamesh epic parallels the biblical Flood in many details – resting on a mountain, the dove.[101]

In a schema of related concepts[102], the daidalon, what is made, is not only a taking apart and putting together in an arrangement of the parts of the animal in sacrifice (as above), but from Homer, an assembling, as in the building of a ship, as much as it is a weaving, as of the ship's sails (pteros, the word for a bird, or a bird's wings), the oars its feathers; a carpenter or boat builder is tecton, from tikto, as above; histos is both mast and the loom's upright. The word for weaving is hyphanein, to make appear, and, wearing her new peplos, nine months in the weaving, the ancient wooden statue of the goddess Athena appeared annually, drawn through the city in a boat-like carriage.

The ship procession of Athena may have been a development from a similar procession of Dionysos[103], the god who arrived from the sea (and an echo of the Egyptian procession of gods' statuary on the Nile).

> The staging of Part 2 continues to be in the open space with the audience, but, though the ship is only in the language, has become the procession. The actors displace together, and they look literally forwards.

If we're not in history yet, we're in its construction. We are following the stories, and this one is the Voyage.

As you head north at night, the constellation of the Great Bear reaches down towards the horizon.

> On the far northwest side of the dark water, at the mouth of the Danube lies nowadays Romania, and the river leads up into the Carpathian Mountains. This is a strange way home for Jason, who could have headed more easily through the Hellespont directly to the Aegean Sea and his home in northern Greece. But he is giving the Colchians the slip, or maybe he just has to mark that Zodiac, or lay claim to a few outposts. In ancient times (not unconnected to its modern superstition) this area was home to a wolf cult (Lykos, wolf) with cannibalistic overtones[104]. A number of names tell similar stories: Lycourgos did not welcome Dionysos, and was punished by going mad and dismembering his son. The dark side of sacrifice. Pausanius[105] tells of an entirely real boy who was turned into a wolf in the kingdom of Arcadian Lykaon, and slaughtered.

What might Medea hear in this new north?

Similarly, in Euripides' *The Bacchae*[106], we see Pentheus (meaning the one who suffers) hunted and torn apart by the Bacchae (Maenads), including his mother Agave in her frenzy, for refusing to accept the Dionysian cult and spying on them from a treetop in a woman's dress. But Kerenyi,[107] contradicting Nietzsche, sees Pentheus as an aspect of Dionysos in his essential doubleness: the god who dies and returns as a child from the sea, spending the intervening year in the underworld. This is a quite different picture to Burkert's bloodthirsty night, exclusive to men, of Zeus Lykaion. But still, the victim of the sacrifice is the god.

> *Actual killing lay at the heart of the most ancient ritual, though its later forms had a theatrical aspect.*[108]*, But the distinction blurs. In a ritual, apparently representational though it may be, the event happens again. Or, this is that. It is the loss of this 'again' that freezes myth, fixes its forms.*

> *Game: the form empty for happening. One in each Part. In The Medead, the same as a ritual.*

> *The agon of the athlete in the game was compensation for the sacrifice.*[109]

> *Foreshadowing: see micro- and macrocosm; its opposite is "again".*

And on, to ice, and fragmentation, and ending.

As a poet, fragments made sense to me. In Guy Davenport's translation of the *Fragments of Archilochus*[110], what could be clearer than the narrative of

Wine
[   ]
Concerns
[   ]
Weeps
[   ]
Inclines
[   ]
Crash

Who needs all the adjectives and particles and grammar? And in

arou[nd]
toward Thasos
[   ] accomplishment

might not arou- equally become arouse? Why not both? In the fragments
of Greek novels[111],

] they
] unless each
] both
] And to me
] an instruction [
] sister [
] s/he said [
] s/he bore and conversing
] much worse than it/he [
]   [
] ordered [
] and by force [
] of the lovers [
] eye of love [

reminds at the beginning of Clark Coolidge's use of prepositions, essential
relation, as in[112]

is so
of
from

or of Nathalie Sarraute's plays, in which all is relation, and the supposed
substance, for example of *The Lie*[113], beside the point. Anne Carson's choice
not to fill in the gaps between the fragments in her Sappho translations[114]
leaves them as intense distillations of language aerated with possibility.

Shattering: a multiplication, fragmentation or rather refraction; dazzling,
connected to invisibility or rather un-see-ability; scattering as seed or sperm;
connected to the moment of change, including in sacrifice; body-parts; sceni-
cally, the differentiation of aspects of characters, sometimes called "split";
repetition in space or time of a scenic trope, exactly or in microcosm/macro-
cosm; echo or unison of a sound, often at an "Oh"; moments of multiplicity
of person, or meaning. It becomes literal, spatial and sonic. Shudder, as in
the moment of ecstasy or sacrifice.

This language is both strange and possible. It is spoken as if it were natural, but its difference to known speech should not be domesticated; multiple possibilities of meaning are all there, and its rhythms are written in single and double linebreaks. In rehearsal, the words are shattered and reassembled.

And melting again, and beginning again,

in the northern part of their spiral journey, in Hyperborea, beyond the dawn, Greek for the far north. The *Medead* is both epic and of course Me Dead. Medea's journey is a 'night sea crossing', a descent of the soul, as Inanna in Mesopotamia, Proserpine-like, goes down to Hell[115], of the Styx ferrying in Roman myth, or the Egyptian Book of the Dead[116]. But the journeys typical of the dead were also shared by ecstatics; in Georgia, "with remnants of Persian Mazdaism", girls "known as *messulethe*" fall into trance to accompany the dead and speak in their voices[117]. *Suli* is a soul.

The repetition in Inanna is clearly rhythmic, therefore spoken:

From the summits of heaven
she looked into the pit
She was a god on the summits of heaven
but her heart was in hell
...
This lady left earth and heaven
and went down into the pit
...
She left in Nippur, Baratushgarra,
she went down into hell.
Eulmash she left in Agada
down to hell she walked away.

In the time of the poem we move with her. The repetition is the duration of action. It is intensifying, emphatic, a dance.

Geshtinanna in Mesopotamia searched for her brother Dumuzi, as Isis in Egypt wandered looking for Osiris her castrated and dismembered brother and lover, as Ishtar searched for Tammuz, as Aphrodite and the dead boy Adonis[118], as Dionysos and Semele[119]. The dismembered brother Apsyrtus has echoes.

By the time the Argo reappears in the Mediterranean from its unlikely voyage across the Alps, we have crossed time too. Medea seems to be endlessly pre-birth, if not necessarily pregnant, by now "eggs on knife-edge" in an Easter breakfast sacrifice, played with evangelical chorus.

In the Argonautika, Orpheus sings the storm-caught ship through the strait of the sirens[120]. Singing women, why would that be alien to him? Because he is the book, the differentiated, and not in fact the singer. He needed to deflect the danger of the voice from the hearer.

Medea is fine with women who sing.

In my first few trials at speaking into a tape recorder as a form of producing "writing"[121], I first generated descriptions of hypnogogic imagery; then language came in, seen and heard. I wrote it in quotation marks, as if outside of myself, at least not as a rationally owned thought. This aspect became increasingly what I wanted to understand. Consciously, I entered into the landscapes, shifting visually from one subject-position to another, as one does in dreams. Jung, in *Aspects of the Feminine*[122] , suggests the question: "'Why do you want this?'...one should cultivate the art of conversation with oneself in the setting provided by an affect, as though the affect itself were speaking." So I asked. At first we spoke in two languages, my rational one, and these fragments I was producing, clashes of morphemes, tips of icebergs. Then we spoke together, and multiplied, and I had found the language of *The Medead*.

In *The Medead*, the choric dialogue with the sirens, like Medea's first conversation with her father, like the scene in her first encounter with Jason and Orpheus where her hands speak to each other, like the katacrypt scene in Corinth, is from this early form of dialogue, the different voices melting back and forth into each other.

As the covering that makes appear with the glimmer of its texture, these fragments wove the form of a world; or as a developing polaroid comes slowly to light.

At a certain stage of the writing, or speaking, in the corn crib studio, my day would be a cycle of speaking into a tape recorder; transcribing; and reading; and speaking again. As I transcribed I would sometimes wonder what I had meant, if I had meant, in the sense of intended, anything, by such and such a word or phrase. Then in the subsequent reading, I would find its source, that I hadn't known I knew. So the filtering apparatus of the sources was not always at a conscious level.

While this is not the same as an automatic writing (strange how

291

people assume that abandoning the page is abandoning thinking), it was also not *structured* by thought, thought as a representation of an idea. It was a dense activity of thinking, structured by language.

The siren-women lead to the nurse-women, the wetnurses of Dionysos.

In the Argonautika there is no such episode, but instead two visits bookend the siren scene: one to Kirke, of the famous magic powers that held Odysseus and his sailors captive in the Odyssey, and sister to Aeetes; Kirke, out of family duty, recruits Thetis, goddess of the sea, to help her niece stay safe on the voyage, but repudiates Medea for her actions. Then they arrive on Drepane, where Queen Arete advises Jason and Medea that if they sleep together that night, King Alkinoos will accept their marriage , and so defend them against the Colchians taking back Medea. The Argonauts make a sacrificial feast, and the couple bed down on the fleece, its glow making the nymphs' cheeks blush, in the cave of Makris, and are saved in the morning. Makris was the wetnurse of Dionysos in his child form, in the Argonautika said to be chased there by Hera for having put honey to the child's lips[123] (a prelude to suckling); in Ovid the nurses are plural[124], and elsewhere Medea rejuvenated the nurses and their husbands[125]; but surely the secret marriage of Jason and Medea on the fleece has to do with the Dionysiac rebirth ritual; presumably his wetnurses were his Bacchic followers, women renewing his cult. Drepane means sickle, scythe, from drepo, to break off or pluck, and metaphorically, to possess, enjoy. It is the sickle-shaped island, now Corfu, where, Apollonius tells us with coy reluctance, lies buried the sickle used by Kronos to castrate his father Ouranos. Or Demeter's scythe, goddess of harvest, De-Meter. Dionysos in his underworld state was separated from his phallus[126]; and part of the duties of the nurses of Dionysos, or the Maenads, was keeping secret the existence of and the action in the rites surrounding this phallus, referring to it as the child they nursed. The original nurses included his mother, Semele, Ariadne his wife, as well as Makris, the knife. It is all this, and

Medea learns it.

Tragedy may be traced to the visible ritual, and comedy to the secret, Dionysiac ones. Like Hades, like death, like the god, the obscene waits offstage, unseen; till it erupts and carries us off. But comedy was also utopian[127]. Sitwell describes the young men in the rites of the Roman *Lupercalia*, "who were obliged, after they had been sacrificed by proxy, to break into laughter, to show that their sacrifice was completed, and that they had passed beyond death."[128]

Several colonies later, the Mediterranean staked out, home. At least for Jason. In Pasolini's *Medea*, the new ground of Greece is a parched mud, on which she screams in horror, "Where are the gods?"

Part 3
Medea in Iolcos
(myth and anthropology)

In Volos, the nearest contemporary Greek city to where Iolcos might have been, the site is said to be lost, but buses nevertheless head up the winding wooded mountain roads that hood the town, with the destination of Iolkos written across their brows, up towards Mount Pelion, with its dark timber architecture and roofs like fishscales. This Iolkos, tucked below a hill, has a Mycenean ruin; though prehistoric Dimini has larger tombs and houses, and lays claim to the ancient name. In the dim Museum of Volos, case after case displays hundreds of tiny Neolithic figures, and on a hot ridge further up the mountain is Sesklo, dating to 6000BC, where fishbones were found. The place shifts, the view remains, with its entering ships.

> Iolcos is played on a hierarchical plane, though not yet on a stage. Perhaps it is in the seats with the audience onstage, perhaps on a balcony. The audience look up as to the hills.

Home, laughing like thunder, his sign, Jason has his exploits celebrated in character-istically cryptic fashion by another feast-song from Orpheus.

> While his story is in most versions of the voyage of the Argonauts, it is in Pindar[129] that we most splendidly see Jason, appearing like a stranger full-grown, his golden curls rippling down over the lion-skin on his back, flexing muscle in the market-place. Only King Pelias recognises him, at least as an enemy, from an oracle that said he should beware of a stranger wearing only one sandal. Jason has supposedly lost his, as he came down Mount Pelion, in a stream, carrying across an old woman who turns out to be his patron goddess, Athena.

> > But the wearing of one shoe, though perhaps the sign of a fighting man (for purchase)[130], is also a sign of the shaman. In Dogon cul-ture[131], the limp, like the stutter, shows that the person participates partly in the other world. Hephaestus had a limp[132] from being twice thrown to earth from heaven. This appearing and disappearing is the performed fragment, the presence of the fragment. It is the

293

flickering world. The Scots word for limp, *hirple*, also means to dance. Hobbling makes a circle, runs round hills, like Achilles three times undoing the walls of Troy.

Fragment: in speech, at several points, a speaking partly in another time; a kind of shattering within language; another is a spraying, connected to the regenerative moment; another is the partial speech. The visible part of what is in the other world

"..drops his shoulder, as if under the weight of a huge bird"[133].

Jason was raised by the centaur Cheiron, having been hidden from Pelias as a child, when Pelias usurped the throne from Jason's father. Cheiron, part horse, and a healer, taught the child the world. Now Pelias calls the young newcomer the son of a whore and to get rid of him sends him on, he imagines, the fruitless quest for the fleece. This is the Argonautika story.

Having told, Orpheus' task too is done. So after a backward glance he withdraws to the mountain to his own ecstasy, to be torn apart, ascetic that he is, by the sensual and wild female followers of Bacchus, and to become the talking head,

in the divergence of book and song.

Perhaps[134] the advent of writing is the end of the meeting of men and gods, retreated into "the silence of the mind"; and Orphism a deadly ascetic legalism. Euripides' Theseus scorns Hippolytus for his interest in Orpheus and his "books of arcane absurdity"[135]. But if what is actually worshipped is life itself [136], the gods have not gone; they are simply lurking in the bushes.
Which is where comedy begins[137].

But in the early 20th century anthropological reading of myth, the brothers Aeson and Pelias are two versions of the sacred king[138]. Elsewhere the original golden fleece is described as purple[139], and a rite was still performed on Mt Pelion in historical times, of the symbolic killing of an old man in a black sheepskin, then revived by companions in white fleeces. For him, this is the aging king sacrificed at the close of his reign, and brought back as the young king. Or the ritual on Mount Pelion may be an expiation by the sacrificers, identifying with their victims to the point of wearing their skins[140]. Or the killing may be an agrarian rite[141], like the cyclical folk songs of John Barleycorn who must be killed (drunk) and buried, the seed that will grow to a plant, then is thrashed (threshed), fermented and drunk. But the grape's property of fermentation is also a further image of life generating, and the wildness of Dionysos' attendant rites, particularly at his reappearing, an expression of pure *zoe*, life. So the vine and the drink are not the ends of the story but the symbols and embodiments of a more transcendently experienced worship. In sacrifice, killing is not for the purpose of death. It is generative.[142]

> *Rejuvenation: on narrative level, just that. At the heart of each of the six parts of the piece. Passage, often within the piece, sought differently to how it is realised. The double arrow of time, both becoming older and younger, born or dead. The several Medeas are of course also the simultaneity of this.*

If Medea rejuvenates Aeson, it is because Jason has come back. In the *Medead*, this rejuvenation works, because it is Jason and Medea's sexual negotiations and coming together. Who is now the father?

> How though could Pelias' rejuvenation work? His daughter is Alcestis[143], wife of Admetus. Such a man couldn't be king, and such a marriage could not rejuvenate the old king. Admetus doesn't want to die, so expects others to do so for him—his parents he asks first, insultingly, then accepts that his wife will. She does. In Euripides' *Alcestis*, Heracles goes to the underworld to bring her back[144]. But according to Apollodorus, it was the young queen of the underworld, Kore (Persephone's name while below), who sent her back, not accepting her death. For Calasso, Admetus is the king of the dead himself[145].

> *Split: See Breathing; and Ambiguity. The shape of Part 3. Admetus and Alcestis play the corrupt versions of Jason and Medea's actions. And Pelias is Aeson playing his own opposite.*

Ovid, for Iolcos, relishes the recipe of a full-fledged witch with reptile-parts, entrails, sleight of hand, and cauldron, forerunner of Shakespeare's weird sisters. The cauldron was an important sacrificial implement[146], but the tale in Ovid also has one of those strange slippages from the living to the artifice: Medea is said to put a real ram in the cauldron, then show the image of a lamb to pretend she knows how to rejuvenate; this reminds of Pasiphae on Crete hiding behind the image of a cow to have sex with the bull she loves. I doubt if anyone was fooled, but we hover in a theatricalisation of the cult object.

> In these stories, Medea has been disappearing again. She is not history, even if maybe (as object) its cause. All of this surrounds her.

In the *Medead* I give this subject its voice(s).

The truth is, she doesn't have to do much. These rejuvenations are taking care of themselves. But, accused of crime again, Jason and Medea flee again.

Part 4
Medea in Corinth
(the psychological world)

> The audience return after an interval, to take the conventional audience seating. The shape of the Corinth staging is vertical.
>
> *Microcosm-macrocosm: the relation, scenically, of 2nd to 1st acts; also, of many foreshadowings, play within play etc; and refractions to many. The movement between them can be spiral, as in the shape of Parts 2 & 6. Change of scale, as in the surface of the body as the theatre of war.*

She lies there. What she is in the middle of here is everything that can happen, has happened, will happen, should happen, must not happen, or be done.

> A story once told exists, whether or not it is disproved. In theatre, what is shown, lie though we know it to be, is what has taken body, what has not only happened but existed. This is the most difficult of the six parts to hold back from "See there! see there!"[147] So there is no Jason in the Corinth of *The Medead*, and no children. No nurse, no-one but Medea. Even the birds and chorus are, as for the first Medea of the Prologue, what she hears.
>
> And this Medea speaks her own titles. Enough men have spoken for her.

Euripides' *Medea*, and after him Seneca's even more so, begin in media res. We don't see Medea *discover* Jason's unfaithfulness, or his desire for the throne. They are, for those plays, facts, and the question is what to do; which their audiences know already. So the plays are the nuances and pain of a passion full-blown, to that point, infanticide, which we watch coming like a train wreck. Gilbert Murray, wishing against hope for an intervention, realises that Medea is instead her own dea ex machine.[148]

How did we get here?

> "From at least the early 5th century BC, Medea was represented by the Greeks as a complex figure, fraught with conflicting desires and exhibiting an extraordinary range of behaviour. In this regard, she differs from most of the other figures we meet in Greek myth, who present far simpler *personae*."[149]

Most literary historians agree that there is no single Medea. The helper-maiden of Colchis is not this rage. Euripides has Medea take full responsibility for the dragon's death, but why would she? So that he can put into her mouth the words, "I killed", repeated twice in that speech to Jason[150].

She is in all stories not Greek[151]. But that can mean just from another part of Greece. The more Greece became Greece, the further away Medea was from. In any case, woman, foreign, complex, clever, dark (in Pindar an Egyptian Colchian; and there were Colchians in Libya. The Amazons were also supposed to be from her region[152]). A woman was already a threat to the stability of the household, coming from outside. An image of the worst was necessary, as caution to the enemy within household and state. But that's Part 5.

Ancient Corinth looks out to a wide bay, as if you can see in many directions at once, across to Delphi, even out to the distant sea.

In the museum at Delphi, where Apollo's shrine stood, I kept wondering what the object identified as the omphalos, the navel of the earth, looked like; a bee-hive they say, but my eyes finally saw it as an egg in a net. But this is a later recreation; the original is ancient and there is, so to speak, nothing to see.
At Delphi the Sibyl, the oracle, was described as a bee, sweet with honey and sound. Like birds, bees are winged and whispering. But she was Pytho, the snake too, whispering and curling like smoke, envenomed, unfixed.

But Corinth is no shifting speculation; ancient, Hellenic and Roman layers stretch across this one place. A refuge from the sun, the so-called spring of Glauke is splashed with red, no doubt from its guarding tree; it is a huge formless stone into which a pillared portico has been incongruously built, and leads downwards, out of reach of permission. Pasolini's Glauke ran in flames along the massive walls of the Akrocorinth, soaring some kilometers away, site for female deity cults. In the Museum, after rooms of mostly stolid Romans, we come to the finds from the Asklepion, the temple of the physician Asklepios. To be cured, the patient had to sleep there and dream[153]. Dismembered ears, limbs, uteri, feet of all sizes, breasts, penises, hang in rows, ancient terracotta offerings of thanks for cure.

Medea of Corinth is the one people say they know, as they "know" a person in a story or a play and ascribe to them feelings and thoughts not in the text.

What is the worst woman? What is not a woman? Is it the woman who kills her children? Is that the same as a woman who kills a man's children? Not for the man, though it may be the same person. What is a woman who is not a mother? What is a woman who speaks? What is a woman who knows? Agave tore her son apart and came home with his head on a stick[154]. Yet we remember Medea. Myth is full of men who killed their children. It is also full of parricides. Heroes in general kill other men.

She is listening, to the world, to children, to herself; perhaps they are the same thing. She speaks to them, to "him". They fill her head. She sings. She gathers her blood, on a torrent of red. Something must be done.

A cluster of words refer to the nature of seeing in sacred mysteries: *myeo*[155] (the root of the word), which is to close, "as the eyes do after seeing", suggesting to close oneself, or upon something, as a secret; *epopteia*, the state of having seen, which he identifies as a result also of watching a tragedy, specifying that Aristotle's catharsis was not from intellectual learning from what the performance showed, but achieved through an actual experience; and the seeing of the vision itself, *autopsia*. It is curious that for us the word for seeing for oneself is now used only for examination of a corpse.

Muo as in myesis is also to close the mouth, to fall silent, after not only seeing in a special way but speaking in a special way[156]; so mythos describes the execution of speech-acts. The word *drao*, to do, from which our drama, is to perform within a tragedy, but also in the real world to sacrifice. Both of these notions, *muo* and *drao*, have lost part of their reality for us, a doubleness that remains however in our own use of the same word for two apparently different activities: to act, in the Hegelian sense, to do something which commits in the world; yet ironically it also describes the pretence, the becoming-another of theatre. So too the word *appearing*, active presence, now also means to seem, that is to present a visual aspect that could be false.

One supposed distinction between performance art and theatre is that the first is actually doing, arising from the history of making, and that the second is pretending to do. And yet the activity of the body is real. To do and to make are the same words in many languages. The difference must then be in, what, the subject? If I see two subjects speak to each other, that may not be the subjects of the people from whose mouths the words come, can those people be lying if the dialogue moves forwards, happens? What does it mean for their bodies? Or their subjectivities? What is it for a woman to play Euripides or Seneca's Medea? As that Medea combs through her reasons, who decides to act?

In all of my performance and installation works, there is a hole. Where making is no longer needed, or no longer appropriate, or can only resolve in the entry of the other subject, and I let go; to the performers or to the audience. And then I take it again, but of necessity differently. In *The Medead*, I wondered where this is. In each Part there is something the audience does not, as such, see. In Corinth, though the speaking continues, I allowed myself not to see.

By the time the Medea of Colchis, of the Panhellenic epic, came to Corinth, the site already had a complex myth[157]: that Hera, the classical mother goddess who had a shrine there, bade her hide her children underground; or Medea hid her children from the Corinthians; or the Corinthians killed her children. Any of these could correspond to an initiation rite, from one life-stage to another, of which Medea certainly had considerable practice: Aeson and Pelias, the nurses of Dionysos and by extension Dionysos himself; possibly Apsyrtus (whose name may also mean[157] "unshorn", not yet adult); and later Theseus. Or not. It is the jealous goddess Hera who was not only a goddess of mothers (different to a mother-goddess), but paradoxically known for visiting death or ill-health on the children of those whom her husband Zeus had fallen for. Zeus loved Medea, and though she spurned his advances, Hera refused Medea's plea for the health of her children, resulting in Medea's hiding them, *katakryptein*, to hide *down*. Was Medea being faithful to Jason? Or to another god? Her children did not, like Kore, come back from hiding below.

Down goes Medea, speaking to children we can't see.

I'm not presenting an alternative person. Rather a figure that glitters alive in the language and in those gaps, in the translation of ear to sight; of metaphor to deed; of actors to embodiments.

Near Corinth lies Lamia, name of another reputedly malicious female, said to lure young men to kill them. This[158] is a reproductive demon; a folk-figure; and reproductive demons are usually women who die without having reared a healthy child, returning with malicious intent against the children of others. Lamia's children by Zeus were taken live from her womb by Hera. So a terrifying statue of her was erected at Corinth to keep the reproductive demons away. Johnston tells us too of the phenomenon in other cultures - Chihuacohuatl, who always carries a papoose pack; a peek inside reveals an Aztec sacrificial knife. Her contemporary figure is La Llorona, protector of mothers without child, weeping her way across the world in search of hers.

Is the statue, the made thing, the Lamia? The thing we must not look on? At the end of Keats' *Lamia* we hardly feel that the tutor has done the hero her lover a favour by pointing out the illusion she offers (he also does not tell us exactly what lies behind the illusion — is that not fear itself of the made-real, the theatrical?).

Medead has shed now, as she wished as a girl.

Medea goes up, speaking to a woman we can't see. Perhaps it is a mirror.

Glauke — the glint of water or the eye — whom Jason wants to marry. But that's if we follow Euripides' take, which might have been written[159] to give history a sunnier view of the infanticidal Corinthians. Let's talk, though, of the burning cloak Medea sends her as a marriage gift. It is golden, or perhaps purple. Fire-like colours we know, desirable and lethal, it was woven by the Graces for Dionysos as his love-couch with Ariadne, and given to Medea by Jason who had received it from Hypsipile, queen of Lemnos; the women of Lemnos killed all their men, but the queen slept with Jason on his way to Colchis and asked him to keep this token when she let him get away. Of course he didn't keep it, but had Medea send it to Apsyrtus to lure him to his death[160]. So again it is her weapon. But there are other cloaks and coverings —the cloak Jason wore on arriving at Lemnos, made for him by Athena, described, like Heracles' cloak, like Achilles shield, as more of a world than a garment. The dazzling of any emergence in the made thing. You could even hear music in it. These coverings do not stand still. Medea makes such things. Who then made Glauke appear? Now you see her, and now her father covers her, but the flames hold him. Another dad down, another throne lost for Jason. Appropriately he is killed by a speaking mother — not Medea, but the falling mast of his ship, made from the speaking oak of Dodona. *"Thus did the Argo shout in the darkness."*[161].

From there, for Medea, the train is without brake. She exits in foreign costume, with dragons[162]. In Euripides, not in *The Medead*, that is. Either way psychology does not win out.

But despite all the complexities accruing to the figure of Medea, her enduring fascination is "the stark fact of her infanticide"[163].

> Though we don't need to see it, (or rather, what I show is unseen), I won't take Medea's knives away. Or her red. They are in her speech from the very beginning. Whether or not Medea, there are the multiple projections of fear.

Part 5
Medea in Athens
  (the political world)

> Athens is played on a tiny triangle of light, the two then three performers struggling for foothold and front.

> Athens is the west. Athens is now.

Aegeus means goat, another sacrificed king, who yet again wants a rejuvenation from Medea, or as he thinks of it, to solve his problem of childlessness. Euripides thought him important enough to her story to show up in his *Medea*. Why? It hardly seems enough of a reason that his visit is to ask her as an expert in such matters, to solve the riddle of the oracle he has just visited about his problem; and that he offers her refuge in return, should she ever need it[164]. There are no other extraneous characters in the play. The Roman Seneca cuts him out. But he is a voice of respect, the only one, contrasting with Creon's and Jason's invective.

And here she is in Athens, and Aegeus wants an heir.

> Some stories say that he gets it, and that Medea's son Medeius is his (in Hesiod her child by Jason), the one who founded the Medes, Theseus' great enemies, though they must have existed before. She is also said to have cured the madness of Herakles[165] while in Athens.

This Medea's voice is weary.

But here comes Theseus, a crashing arrival at the party. Just what she needs, right?

Arrival: the coming of what has not been present; see passage. Re-placing. Arrival has to be acknowledged, is its acknowledgement (eg Theseus arrives several times unsuccessfully until he is recognised); change; the return of the god from below. Arrival is not always visible. But appearing is a form of arrival.

In Ovid's Metamorphoses[166], Theseus is fresh from killing a series of bad guys, on his way to get what he can. He recently, now old enough to lift a certain rock and find Aegeus' sword hidden, found out that he was conceived one forgotten drunken night, and that Aegeus is his father. In Plutarch[167] Theseus is the founder of Greece as a unified state and the first democracy, though rule by the people was rule by certain people only, certainly not foreigners, who were massacred or expelled. Medea is the image of the focus of his genocidal project. Shakespeare's Theseus makes fun of the theatrical efforts of the rude mechanicals; not one to be enthralled. He wants to see the play after being told "it is nothing, nothing in the world". Shakespeare knew the value of that nothing.

In Florence I looked at frescoes unable to be fully restored, the images partly revealed behind plaster; to me these non-images were great puffs of unknown, ascending stairs, entering the room, companions, blotting heaven, or being heaven. The incomplete multiplied the possible spaces within the real.

In Samita Sinha's music, there is no drone in Athens, no thread holding the world. Musical devices included a car alarm, a fuzzy PA announcer, radio, loose mikes being dragged.

The choric breathing and birds give way to "the sound of choppers".

As usual there's a ritual of male passage. Aegeus wants rid of the aggressive stranger, and Medea concocts the appropriate poison. He'll drink whatever's going, and will be the one to strike the blow on the animal. As he pulls out his sword Aegeus recognises him and greets him. Medea is over for both. She is treated as a murderess, though she probably knew what was coming. Theseus is right. They are enemies. A man just as self-seeking and horny as Jason, and far more violent. Things will be how he says they are.

An impressive number of black vase paintings show Theseus, with bare sword or dagger, naked or clothed, pursuing the fleeing and suppliant Medea[169].

Recognition: partly Aristotelian peripety. Often containing a temporal delay and a change in meaning, paradigm shift; its reversal can also happen - unrecognition or de-recognition, though not truly reversible, wilful ignorance. Related to foreshadowing. Also connected to the multiple actors playing single parts, and the single actors playing multiple parts. Their other identities don't quite disappear.

His job now is to stop the killing of young Athenians as a gage to Minos King of Crete. Of course he is enemy of that past, those foreigners from whom Greece has taken so much. The familiar story is that he kills the half-bull half-man at the centre of a labyrinth. The labyrinth, a turning, a dance, as on Achilles' shield[170]. But of course, it is Ariadne who helps him find his way with her thread wound through its spirals. Her half-brother, the bull, dead (also a figure of her future husband Dionysos, the bull, the roarer, Bromio another of his names), Theseus takes her then abandons her. The labyrinth was created by Daedalus; how can one weave a thread through a spiral shell? Daedalus knew—he tied it to the leg of an ant. Ant, Theseus, both betrayed Daedalus the maker.

In a term similar to the notion of chaos as *aporia*, without measure, *desmoi apeirones* was used for the inextricable bonds of the net made by Hephaestus; and *apeiros* for the labyrinth[171]. The making of the dance is the way out.

> And yet the labyrinth is unseeable. And a dance can not be grasped, but is pursued.

And Aegeus, seeing the ship return with a black sail, recognises the sign that Theseus is dead, and leaps off a rock. Oops. Theseus forgot to change it to white. Who's history now?

Part 6
Medea returns to the east
(the world shifts)

This journey goes back, goes on. Thread spiralling in the ear,
down time, revisiting again and again a bringing to life. Others'.

> Like Demeter herself, searching witless for her lost Kore, her daughter, her other self [172], stolen by Hades, god of the unseeable. Like the sisters for the brothers, the mothers for their children or none.

The other self on film wanders too, child older than mother, her map, her long time of tears. She moves through the ruins of totalitarian occupation. The final Medea moves slowly into the flat plane of the film, completing this history of performance's distance from its audience.

In Part 6, the titles fall away, into presence.

I was asked, what does Medea's mother have to do with it? (With what?) This isn't history. Or even literary history. Medea's mother has death to do with it. Where the birds are, and name was, and purple violet is the sky before the sun. At least this is hers.

Epilogue
The marriage of tears

At the end of the story of being dead, she is all the Medeas.

Medea's posthumous marriage to Achilles is foretold in the Argonautika[173]. How negative can the ancient view of her have really been? They have found the one most like her[174].

War and love, west and east, blade and birth are, rather idealistically, reconciled.

From her map of weeping, Medea in *The Medead* meets Achilles fresh from the end of the *Iliad*, finally letting flow his tears. Tears cover and multiply the looker. She is dazzled by what she sheds.

I de-theatricalised the performance of the final 6-part *Medead*, to stay in the multiple of language and sound, and to let the eyes close a moment, or catch the performers slipping in and out of acting. But I spatialised it, for the same reason and for the body, a world appearing.

~~~

Fiona Templeton
London
December 2013

Sources:

[1]   John Keats, *Lamia,* Part 2 229-30. In *Complete Poems and Selected Letters,* Modern Library 2001.

[2]   Pier Paolo Pasolini dir. *Medea,* film. Vanguard studio, Italy 1969.

[3]   Indra Kagis McEwen, *Socrates' Ancestors.* MIT 1993.

[4]   Aristophanes, *The Birds.* Greece, 5th century BC.

[5]   Farid ud-Din Attar, *The Conference of the Birds.* Persia 12th century.

[6]   Geoffrey Chaucer, *The Parlement of Foulys.*

[7]   This and its opposite phrase, wingless or unuttered, *apteros muthos,* are the subject of much discussion but I'm convinced by this distinction, spoken or not, and therefore addressed or not, in an oral poetry, as in e.g. *A Commentary on Homer's Odyssey Vol II Books X-XIV,* Heubeck & Hoekstra, Oxford 1989, p175.

[8]   *Echoes of Egyptian Voices - an anthology of Ancient Egyptian poetry,* tr. Foster. Univ of Oklahoma Press 1992. p11.

[9]   "The Preface to the Reader", in *Chapman's Homer—The Iliad.* ed. Allardyce Nicoll Princeton Bollingen 1956.

[10]   Rig Veda I XIII 9. p8. intro. Pelikan, Book of the Month Club 1992, from tr. & ed. Griffith, 1889 Motilal Banarsidass publishers

[11]   Although the vowel e in these etymologies shifts from ε to η, there is no absolute divide in meanings.

[12]   Greek dictionaries used are primarily the Follet, Chicago 1929; and Liddell & Scott, Oxford 1940.

[13]   M. Senard, *Le Zodiaque,(clef de l'ontologie appliqué a la psychologie).* Editions Traditionnels, Paris 1948, reprinted 1984. p421.

[14]   from *Mzetamze.* Traditional Music of Georgian Women, CD Berlin 1993.

[15]   Citing Vera Bardavelidze, *The Oldest Religious Concepts and Ritual Graphic Art of the Georgian Tribes,* Tbilisi 1957.

[16]   Introduction to *The Gaelic songs of Mary Mcleod,* ed. Watson. Blackie & Son, Glasgow 1934 pp xi-xvii.

[17]   Heidegger, *Building, Dwelling, Thinking,* p.159, cited in McEwen p.146.

[18]   Pindar *The Odes, (Pythian IV),* 6th century BC. tr C.M. Bowra, Penguin 1969. 11 p188.

[19]   *Assyrian Reliefs and Ivories in the Metropolitan Museum of Art,* fig 16. New York 1980.

[20]   Illustration in *The Ancient Near East, vol II,* (plates 88,89) ed. Pritchard, Princeton 1975.

[21]   Illustration in the New York Review of Books, of *Art of the First Cities: The Third Millenium BC from the Mediterranean to the Indus,* exhibition at the Museum of Modern Art, New York 2003.

[22]   H.R.E. Davidson, *Myths and Symbols in Pagan Europe.* Syracuse University Press 1988 p143.

[23]   Pindar, *Pythian IV,* 77-83.

[24]   Mircea Eliade, *Mythes, Rêves et Mystères,* Part V. Gallimard 1957.

[25]   Apollonius of Rhodes, *Argonautika,* 3rd century BC. as *Jason and the Golden Fleece,* tr. Hunter, Oxford Classics, 1993; and tr. Seaton, Loeb 1988.

[26]   Homer, *Odyssey* XII 70.

[27]   McEwen, p.26.

[28]   Shot'ha Rust'aveli, *The Man in the Panther's Skin,* Georgia 12th century. Tr. Wardrop, London 1912, reprinted Nekeri 2005.

[29]   Richard N. Frye, *The Heritage of Persia.* Weidenfeld and Nicolson 1963.

[30]   Herodotus, *The Histories,* 5th century BC. Tr. Aubrey de Selincourt, Penguin 1963.

[31]   David Braund, *Georgia in Antiquity: A History of Colchis and Transcaucasian Iberia, 550 BC-AD 562* (1994)

[32]   Pindar, *Pythian IV.* 84-5.

[33]   M.L. West, *The Orphic Poems.* Cambridge 1983. pp3-4. Most (not all) of this and the next paragraph cites this source.

[34] Hesiod, *The Theogony.* in *The Works and Days; Theogony; The Shield of Herakles,* tr. Lattimore, University of Michigan 1991.

[35] *Rig Veda,* Book I Hymn LIV p36 n3.

[36] Carl Kerenyi, *Dionysos, Archetypal Image of Indestructible Life,* Princeton/ Bollingen,1976. p119.

[37] Ovid, *Metamorphoses,* Book XV. The Innes translation inserts the name Pythagoras into the text as the speaker, although it does not appear in the Latin, which identifies him as a certain man from Samos, exiled from there for his beliefs. (Penguin, 1955. p336).

[38] See note 33.

[39] *Poems of Heaven and Hell from Ancient Mesopotamia,* tr Sandars. Penguin 1971 pp73-75

[40] *As above,* p75.

[41] Plato, The Republic, 364c-e.

[42] McEwen, p34.

[43] a distinction made by Claude Calame, following Benveniste, in *The Craft of Poetic Speech in Ancient Greece,* tr. Orion, Cornell 1995. p27.

[44] Homer, The Iliad Book 2.

[45] Homer, The Iliad Book 18.

[46] McEwen, p29.

[47] Joseph Campbell, *The Hero with a Thousand Faces, Princeton Bollingen 1968.*

[48] Georgian language information: Georgian-English dictionary, ed Gvardjaladze; & advice from individuals, particularly Levan Khetaguri and Nato Murvanidze.

[49] Frye, pp64-65.

[50] A.T. Olmstead, *History of the Persian Empire,* University of Chicago, 1948. p22.

[51] In the 6th century BC—Olmstead p322.

[52] Firdawsi, The Shahnahmeh, tr Atkinson. Warne & Co 1886 pp40-44.

[53] M. Senard, *Le Zodiaque* pp41-46,68-79. The quotations in this paragraph are from this Source.

[54] *Argonautika,* II 1247-1259.

[55] Graves Vol I p148 (39,8)

[56] *Rig Veda,*I X n2 p6; I XVII nI P10.

[57] *Rig Veda* I XX n6 p11.

[58] Sergei Paradjanov, *The Legend of Suram Fortress,* film, 1984—puppet scene c00:48.

[59] Braund pp28-9.

[60] British Museum. See http://www.mesopotamia.co.uk/tombs/explore/ram.html last accessed 8/23/2013.

[61] *Rig Veda* I XVIII p10 n4 (ed Pelikan).

[62] *Rig Veda* IX CVI 10 p524; IX XXIII 4 p480.

[63] *Rig Veda* X CXXIX & CXXX pp633-4; X CXXV n1 p631.

[64] Ovid, *Heroides,* XII 30. Loeb 144-5.

[65] in the Argonautika.

[66] in Apollodorus, , I,2,1 Hades has a helmet of invisibility.

[67] Ovid, *Metamorphoses Book VI.* tr. Innes pp146-154.

[68] *Ovid's Metamorphosis, Englished, Mythologised, and Represented in Figures,* George Sandys 1632. Facsimile reprint, Kessinger nd p213. & ed. Bush, Univ of Nebraska 1970. (546-7)

[69] Shakespeare, *A Midsummer Night's Dream,* Act III Scene i.

[70] Louis Zukofsky, *Bottom: on Shakespeare.* p21.

[71] Pindar, Pythian IV 214. Penguin Classics p199.

[72] Pindar, Pythian II I-II 21-48. pp147-8.

[73] Graves. Vol I p197 (58.5), Vol II pp236-240 (152).

[74] See note 10.

[75] West p147; Eliade *Shamanism, Archaic Techniques of Ecstasy,* Princeton/Bollingen 1972. pp125,269,487.

[76] Yayoi Kusama made a physically resonant image of this. A ladder stretched from floor to ceiling,

both of which were mirrored, joining the dizzying infinities. *Ladder to Heaven,* Robert Miller Gallery, New York 2003.

[77]   Kerenyi, *Dionysos*, p17.

[78]   *Argonautika* III 619-624.

[79]   *Argonautika* III 853.

[80]   *The Chambers Dictionary*, 1993 edition.

[81]   EV Rieu, introduction to *The Voyage of the Argo,* Penguin 1959 p22.

[82]   Apollodorus, *The Library of Greek Mythology*, date contested—2nd century BC to AD. Oxford Classics tr. Hard 1997. p 54.

[83]   Putkaradze, T. *The Kartvelians*, Kartvelian Heritage 2005. Translation by I.Kutsia online at www.putkaradze.ge/qartvelebi/qartvelebi/links/7.inglis.doc. Last accessed Sept 26 2013.

[84]   *Argonautika* 3 245. Loeb pp210-11.

[85]   Graves 89.9 I p303; & 42.d I p156.

[86]   K.E. Krafft, *Typocosmy,* Verlag Zenith, Dusseldorf 1934, cited in Senard. p79.

[87]   G. Nagy, *Pindar's Homer*. Johns Hopkins 1990 p364.

[88]   *Rig Veda* I CLXXXVII p126. n1.

[89]   *The Ancient Near East*, ed. Pritchard. Princeton 1958.

[90]   *Poems of Heaven and Hell from Ancient Mesopotamia,* p25.

[91]   as above p73.

[92]   as above p32.

[93]   McEwen pp126-128.

[94]   *Poems of Heaven and Hell from Ancient Mesopotamia* p75.

[95]   Graves, Vol II p258 (158,3.)

[96]   Homer, *The Iliad*. tr Robert Fagles, Penguin Classics 1990. (Book 2, 957 & glossary p659)

[97]   Adrian Room, *Dictionary of Placenames, McFarland & Co* 2006 p59.

[98]   Follett, def.

[99]   Graves Vol II p221-3 (148.9-13)

[100]   *The Ancient Near East*, ed. Pritchard. Princeton 1958. Vol I pp28-30.

[101]   *The Ancient Near East*, Vol II. pp64-70.

[102]   McEwen pp64-71, 89-93.

[103]   Kerenyi, *Dionysos*. p167.

[104]   Burkert, pp84-109.

[105]   as above p86.

[106]   Euripides, *The Bacchae*. Loeb 1043-1152.

[107]   Kerenyi, *Dionysos*. p329.

[108]   Burkert p46,76.

[109]   Nagy p148ff.

[110]   *Carmina Archilochai, The Fragments of Archilochus,* tr. Guy Davenport. University of California Press, 1964. 7th century BC

[111]   *Ancient Greek Novels—The Fragments*. ed. Stephens & Winkler, Princeton UP. p337.

[112]   Clark Coolidge, *Space,* Harper & Row 1970.

[113]   Nathalie Sarraute, *The Lie,* in *Silence* and *The Lie*, Calder & Boyars 1969

[114]   Anne Carson, *If Not, Winter*. Vintage 2003.

[115]   "Inanna's Journey to Hell" by the priestess Enheduanna (the first known named poet (R Binkley in Lipson & Binkley, *Rhetoric Before and after the Greeks*, SUNY 2004) in *Poems of Heaven and Hell from Ancient Mesopotamia* pp135-165; tr Sandars, who however does not mention the author—the edition may have preceded the credit.

[116]   *The Egyptian Book of the Dead,* ed. Budge. Barnes & Noble 1951.

[117]   Eliade, *Shamanism*. pp 399-400. Eliade expresses this in the present, but the dating is unclear, as is whether he is using indirect report from older sources.

[118]   see Rose, *A Handbook of Greek Mythology* p224 &n94. Methuen 1953.

[119]   Graves II 124 2,4. pp156-7.

[120] *Argonautika*, IV 885-921.
[121] described in my chapter, "Speaking for Performance, Writing with the Voice", in *Sensualities/Technologies,* eds. Broadhurst & Machon, Palgrave 2009.
[122] Carl Jung, *Aspects of the Feminine,* Princeton/Bollingen 1982 pp89-91.
[123] Kerenyi, *Dionysos.* p31.
[124] Ovid, *Metamorphoses Book VII 294-6.*
[125] West p148.
[126] Graves 27 b,2 pp104-6, & 155 h p252; & Kerenyi *Dionysos.* pp 288-289.
[127] Kerenyi, as above pp342-348.
[128] Edith Sitwell, *A Poet's Notebook,* (US ed) Atlantic Monthly Press 1950.
[129] Pindar, *Pythian IV,* as above.
[130] Graves, 148.14 (II p223).
[131] Nathaniel Mackey, "Sound and Sentiment, Sound and Symbol", in *The Politics of Poetic Form,* ed Bernstein. Roof 1989.
[132] Graves 23 b&1 pp87-88.
[133] Eliade, *Shamanism.* p194.
[134] Roberto Calasso, *The Marriage of Cadmus and Harmony*, tr. Parks, Vintage 1993. pp390,
[135] Euripides, *Hippolytos,* ll 953-54. tr. Bagg, in *The Complete Euripides: Volume III,* Oxford 2009.
[136] Kerenyi, *Dionysos.*
[137] Nagy pp142,390 on the satyric players coming in from the komai, countryside. Also, thanks to Ian Blower in workshop for his Benny Hill interpretation of the satyrs emerging from the bushes.
[138] Graves 14.4. (I p57).
[139] Graves, 148.10 (II p222)
[140] Burkert II, particularly 2, &p98 &n26.
[141] James George Frazer, *The Golden Bough*, Macmillan 1963 (orig. 1922)
[142] Kerenyi, *Dionysos eg* p179.
[143] Apollodorus 1.9,14 (p48)
[144] Euripides, *Alcestis.* 1019-1146. Loeb pp260-279.
[145] Calasso pp72-6.
[146] Burkert II 5.
[147] Cassandra in Aeschylus' *Agamemnon* 1118. Tr. Lattimore. There is no need for us to see, because she has seen for us.
[148] *The Medea,* tr. Gilbert Murray. Oxford UP America 1912.
[149] Clauss, Preface to Clauss & Johnston, *Medea.* Princeton University Press 1997. p7.
[150] Euripides, *Medea. 480-486.* Loeb pp338-9.
[151] Graf, in Clauss and Johnston p38.
[152] Braund, p19; 12-13.
[153] Aristophanes, *Ploutos.* In *Cure and Cult in Ancient Corinth.* American School of Classical Studies at Athens 1977. p13.
[154] Euripides, *The Bacchae* 1139-1142. Loeb p 122-123.
[155] Kerenyi, *Eleusis* pp 46,114.
[156] Nagy pp31-32,66.
[157] Clauss & Johnston pp44-70
[158] as above pp 57 ff.
[159] As above p 45n1.
[160] *Argonautika* I 721-767 pp 20-21 & IV 421-434 p108.
[161] *Argonautika* I 525 Loeb p38-39.
[162] Though the Euripides text is without stage directions, see Sourvinou-Inwood in Clauss & Johnston as above, pp269-271, particularly Plate3.
[163] Edith Hall, "The archetypal anti-mother", TLS Feb 14 1997.
[164] Euripides, *Medea.* 727-8 Loeb pp 362-3.
[165] Graves 135 12. p161

[166] *Metamorphoses*, VII 404-424, Loeb pp370-373..

[167] Plutarch, *The Lives of Noble Grecians and Romans, tr. Dryden & Clough, Modern Library 1992*.

[168] Shakespeare, *A Midsummer Night's Dream*. Act V Scene i.

[169] see Sourvinou-Inwood, "Was Theseus a matricide manqué", in *Bulletin of Classical Studies* Vol 26 Issue S40 pp3-7 Jan1979

[170] McEwen pp57-64.

[171] as above.

[172] Hymn to Demeter, *The Homeric Hymns,* tr Sargent. Norton 1973.

[173] *Argonautika*. IV,805.

[174] Boedeker notes the similarity between the metaphors used for Achilles' heroism and Medea's 'unwomanly' qualities. Clauss & Johnston p129.

~~~

ACKNOWLEDGMENTS

VERY GRATEFUL THANKS TO:

For publishing passages from *The Medead*, or earlier versions: Belladonna chapbooks; call; No; Kiosk; alterra; Object Permanence; Primary Writing; Double Change (French translation by Abigail Lang); WKCR and Penn Sound.

For rhythm, images, sounds, poetics and visions to enter my tongue to speak the work, too many to list, but particularly (in addition to those in the notes) Piero Della Francesca, Biagio d'Antonio's Cassone panels, Minoan & Mycenean Art, Hannah Weiner, William Carlos Williams, William Dunbar. Birds. And the international news.

For performance and performative insights: The Relationship. And in particular Anna Kohler, Stephanie Silver, Robert Kya-Hill, Graziella Rossi, Valda Setterfield, Clarinda MacLow, Peter Sciscioli, Andrew Zimmerman, Dawn Saito, Adam Collignon; and Whitney V. Hunter, Javier Cardona, Tim Hall, Sarah O'Brien, Aysan Celik, Tanya Selvaratnam, Sean Donovan, Drew Cortese, Katie Brown, Julie Troost, Ian Blower, Navraj Sidhu, Dominic Fitch, Caroline Jones, Roberta Kerr, Roy Sadler, Maggie-Meg Reed, Rachel Dickstein, Tom Regan, Black-Eyed Susan, Emma Bernstein.

For discussion and insights: Wendy Walker, Claire MacDonald, Daria Fain, John Jesurun, Siobhan Liddell, Lenora Champagne, Eve Biddle, Robert Kocik, Samita Sinha, Dan Kaufman, Thom Donovan, Ulla Dydo, Gerry Harris, Andrew Quick, Gabriella Giannacchi, Elaine Aston, Anne Carson, Howie Seligman.

For introductions, support, suggestions, translation and hospitality on my visits to Georgia and to Greece: Nato Murvanidze, Nino Gegeshidze Kunin, Julia Kunin, Daniel Kunin, Rismag Gordeziani at the Department of Ancient and Classical Studies of the State University of Georgia in Tbilisi, Levan Khetaguri of the Stichting Caucausus Foundation, Irina Popiashvili, Dan Dzindzihashvili, Claire MacDonald, Deborah Brevoort, Maria Laina, Lizzie Calligas, Katerina Logothetis, Lia Karavia, Aliki Bakopolou-Halls, Maria Triantopolou-Capsaskis and much casual help.

For support for writing time, development workshops and readings: New York State Council on the Arts; The Judith E. Wilson Fund, the English Department, the University Library and Lucy Cavendish College all at Cambridge University, New York Foundation for the Arts, Franklin Furnace, MacDowell Colony, Yaddo, the library at Skidmore College, Virginia Center for the Creative Arts, the library at Sweet Briar College, The Rockefeller Study Center at Bellagio, Fundación Valparaíso, Playlabs Minneapolis, International Women Playwrights' Conference Athens, Lancaster University Department of Theatre Studies, Nuffield Theatre, New York Theatre Workshop, New Dramatists, the Arts & Humanities Research Board, North West Arts, Nicky Childs at Arts Admin, Brunel University, Chisenhale Dance Space, September 11th Fund, Dixon Place, Rachel Levitsky & Erica Kaufman (Belladonna),

Segue Foundation, Byrdcliffe Foundation, Tom White, the Leslie Scalapino—O Books Fund.

For production support: Jim Staley & team at Roulette Brooklyn; Mike Shaver at Governor's Island National Parks Department; Mabou Mines Suite residency; Linda Chapman at NYTW; Steve Slater and team at Tramway in Glasgow, Steffi Jameson at LMCC. For technical insight and help: Eve Biddle, Corina Reynolds, Janelle Iglesias, Janet Clancy, Meredith Holch, Matt Mehlan, Sergei Tcherepnin and Lisa Clair.

For the Afterword, all those in the sources, but for direct quotation particularly Indra Kagis McEwen, ML West, Klaus Kerenyi, M. Senard.

~~~

Samita Sinha

311

Poet and performance maker Fiona Templeton directs the New York performance group The Relationship. She created the 1988 landmark work *YOU–The City*, an intimate Manhattanwide play for an audience of one, and co-founded the Theatre of Mistakes in London in the 70s. Recent productions: *The Medead* at Roulette Brooklyn, on Governor's Island, and at Glasgow Tramway; *L'Ile*, a staging of the dreams of the people of Lille, France, in the places dreamed of; *Flow* by Leslie Scalapino; *Bodies of Memory*, a collective physical remembering of performances from the last 35 years, at Tate Britain.

Her 12 books include *YOU–The City*, *Cells of Release*, *Delirium of Interpretations*, *Elements of Performance Art*. She has received awards and fellowships from the Foundation for Contemporary Performance Arts, NYFA (in both performance and playwriting), the NEA (in both poetry and Visual arts), and a Senior Judith Wilson Writer's Fellowship at Cambridge. She teaches contemporary performance at Brunel University in London.

www.therelationship.org

Claire MacDonald's interests lie at the intersection of fiction, performance and the visual arts. A co-founder of UK visual performance companies Impact and Insomniac, she was a theatre-maker and performer before turning to writing, editing and teaching. A founding editor of the *Journal Performance Research*, she is also a contributing editor to *PAJ: A Journal of Performance and Art* and writes widely on artists and writers whose work crosses genres, as well as on artists' books and publishing, and on the pedagogy of art and performance. Recent writing includes the essay, 'Desire Paths: John Cage's Transatlantic Crossing,' and the book chapter 'All Together Now: Performance and Collaboration' in Dee Heddon and Jennie Klein (eds.) *Histories and Practices of Live Art*, Palgrave 2012. Her collection *Utopia: three plays for a Postdramatic Theatre* will be published in 2014 by Intellect.